# GREAT
# HANDLING RAPID
# CHANGE IDEAS

## Dr Peter Shaw

Marshall Cavendish
Business

Published by Marshall Cavendish Business
An imprint of Marshall Cavendish International

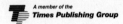
A member of the
**Times Publishing Group**

Other Marshall Cavendish Offices:
Marshall Cavendish Corporation. 99 White Plains Road, Tarrytown NY 10591-9001, USA • Marshall Cavendish International (Thailand) Co Ltd. 253 Asoke, 12th Floor, Sukhumvit 21 Road, Klongtoey Nua, Wattana, Bangkok 10110, Thailand • Marshall Cavendish (Malaysia) Sdn Bhd, Times Subang, Lot 46, Subang Hi-Tech Industrial Park, Batu Tiga, 40000 Shah Alam, Selangor Darul Ehsan, Malaysia

Marshall Cavendish is a registered trademark of Times Publishing Limited

**National Library Board, Singapore Cataloguing-in-Publication Data**

Names: Shaw, Peter, 1949-
Title: 100 great handling rapid change ideas / Dr Peter Shaw.
Description: Singapore : Marshall Cavendish Business, [2018]
Identifiers: OCN 1021801951 | 978-981-4794-63-3 (paperback)
Subjects: LCSH: Organizational change. | Leadership.
Classification: DDC 658.4063–dc23

Printed in Singapore

With thanks to many different companions on
long distance walks for thoughtful conversations
about surviving and thriving through rapid change.

# CONTENTS

## SECTION D: Draw on wise counsel

## SECTION E: Keep learning and growing

## SECTION F: Manage your capabilities

## SECTION G: Evolve your narrative

**LEADING OTHERS**

## SECTION H: Frame of mind

## SECTION I: Balance vision with flexibility of approach

## SECTION J: Keep ahead of the problem

## SECTION K: Listen, communicate and adapt

## SECTION P: Keep the energy high

## SECTION Q: Evolve the narrative

## SECTION R: Thrive with change

## SECTION S: Move to the next mountain

# ACKNOWLEDGEMENTS

I AM PARTICULARLY grateful to Colin, my younger son, for a sequence of stimulating conversations when we talked through ideas for this book. Colin's experience as a consultant with McKinsey means he brings a freshness of approach and a willingness to challenge accepted norms. I have learnt a lot from Colin's clear and insightful thinking.

I am grateful to the many colleagues I worked with in UK Government departments when I was leading on major change programmes—whether that was in education, inner city regeneration, employment policies or tax reforms. The colleagues who influenced me most were those who were excited by the need for change and combined a willingness to explore the consequences of different approaches with an open and energetic spirit and a keen sense of curiosity.

I am grateful to a wide range of individuals and team members I have worked with as a coach who have been addressing major change or leading transformation. I hope I have enabled them to see the prospect of new life and opportunity, however complex or difficult the situation they were addressing.

My thanks go to colleagues at Praesta Partners who have been sources of practical ideas and have always been willing to push my thinking. In particular I want to thank Paul Gray, Hilary Douglas and Una O'Brien for their sound advice and perspective.

I am grateful to Brian Leveson for writing the foreword to this book. Brian has been an inspirational leader to many people and a source of encouragement to me in my work with leaders and teams over the last dozen years.

This book is one of a series of '100 Great Ideas' books that explore personal impact, coaching, team effectiveness, building success and leading well. The books seek to be complementary to each other, enabling the reader to dip into individual chapters and pick up useful ideas. A forthcoming book will address leading through frustration.

Melvin Neo at Marshall Cavendish has been an excellent sponsor of this series. He has always been supportive about my developing ideas for this series. Mike Spilling has been an admirable copy editor of the text.

Jackie Tookey has typed the manuscript with her usual care and efficiency. Tracy Easthope has managed my diary to enable me to have space to write. Together, Jackie and Tracy have been a wonderful support team to whom I owe a great deal.

I am grateful to my elder son, Graham, and my daughter, Ruth, for excellent conversations about what makes people tick and how best to enable people to remain positive through change that can be unsettling. I am very grateful to Frances, my wife, for her encouragement and practical support through all the writing projects.

# FOREWORD

HANDLING RAPID CHANGE is inevitable for every leader. Leading change undeniably requires enthusiasm, flexibility of mind and resilience, along with the ability to inspire confidence and enthusiasm in others. An agile approach and a belief in continuous learning are essential if a leader or manager is going to survive and thrive through rapid change.

Mature leaders confront the need for rapid change with a genuine concern about whether they have the capability and flexibility to change how they work. They should bring a strong sense of humility and healthy apprehension, alongside a commitment to make the right decisions in tough times. Such a leader must bring clarity about what needs to happen alongside a willingness to take tough decisions and the courage to ensure that constructive, sustainable change happens. Key to the process is having the right frame of mind, and the ability to enable and encourage others to view necessary change as inevitable and constructive over the longer term.

Change does not happen easily. It is not linear and there will always be doubters. There will inevitably be problems along the way, with the need to be resolute in pushing forward on an agreed path, as well as adaptable when valid concerns are raised.

Change programmes that are successful and sustainable have been carefully thought through, with a realistic timeline and a communication strategy that operates at a number of different levels. The ultimate goals and benefits are recognizable, with the benefits described in ways that are much more engaging than just cutting costs. Key to building momentum for effective change are visible signs of progress, with early results that are seen as positive. The risk is always that people lose enthusiasm if they cannot see progress.

In recent years I have been involved in helping to generate changes in the way criminal courts operate in England and Wales. The essential elements for progress have included clarity of intent, strong partnership working between different interests, evidence of progress, positive advocates for the changes amongst practitioners, and a willingness to operate in tandem with others.

Peter Shaw brings wide experience of leading through change, initially as a Director General in the UK Civil Service and then working with a wide range of leaders and leadership teams. Over the last dozen years, Peter and I have had many stimulating conversations about leading through change, along with many other aspects of leadership generally. His understanding of the problems and his clarity of exposition and explanation have been invaluable.

This book provides a set of prompts about leading yourself and leading others through rapid change. It is full of practical good sense. I strongly commend the book to any leader or team handling rapid change.

The Rt. Hon. Sir Brian Leveson
President of the Queen's Bench Division
Royal Courts of Justice
London

# INTRODUCTION

HANDLING RAPID CHANGE affects virtually everyone, in whatever sector or country. No one is immune from the effects of technological, political or cultural changes. No leader can afford to resent the changes they need to address.

Handling change effectively is not for the faint-hearted. We need to be able to observe the forces of change around us and be ready to respond. We need to bring a positive belief that out of any change comes learning about ourselves and the possibility of new opportunities.

This book is designed to enable the reader to respond to change in a constructive way and to see opportunities rather than threats. At the heart of learning how to handle change well is being able to understand the context you are in through fresh eyes. Progress comes when we recognise which attitudes or self-beliefs are holding us back and how we can break out of self-limiting and often self-destructive perspectives.

Fundamental to handling rapid change well is leading yourself. In this first section of the book we examine frames of mind, thriving through change, managing fall-out and drawing on wise counsel. Leading yourself includes taking responsibility for your learning, growing your capabilities and evolving your leadership. The second section of the book focuses on leading others, which includes balancing vision with flexibility of approach and keeping ahead of problems. It requires listening, communicating and adapting, as well as building capability, credibility and champions.

The book is designed to give you practical prompts to be able to lead yourself and others with freshness, building a sense of both purpose and curiosity about what the future will hold. It is designed so it can be read either in its entirety or the different sections can be used to provide a thought for a day or a week.

The book includes a number of hypothetical examples of leaders handling rapid change. Alex is an operations manager merging two hospitals. Kim is leading a programme transferring work from Europe to India. Kathy is leading a change programme in an insurance company requiring a one-third reduction in staffing levels. Joe is rationalising the number of premises occupied by a government department. Helen is leading a major IT transformation programme. Bob is leading a major regeneration programme in an inner city. These examples draw from the observed experience of individuals in a range of different contexts. The illustrations exemplify the emotions and practical decisions that need to be addressed by those leading transformation.

Key to handling rapid change successfully is recognising how to maintain your energy levels and keep your mind both focused and open to new information and ideas. I hope this book will help you continue to build your understanding and resilience.

I trust the book will enable you to welcome change and thrive in handling challenges, having updated your narrative and ditched outdated perceptions. My hope is that whatever situation you are in, you will have the opportunity to lead, or contribute to, sustained and constructive change.

Canon Professor Peter Shaw
Godalming
England

LEADING YOURSELF

**SECTION A**
# FRAME OF MIND

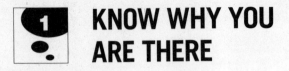

# KNOW WHY YOU ARE THERE

When you are clear why you are in a particular situation you can bring clarity and confidence to your role and contribution.

## The idea

The secret to making a success of any role is to be clear why you are there. Without clarity you can be mesmerised by uncertainty and lack the decisiveness necessary to make a success of what you are there to do. You may have volunteered to be in a role where you are handling rapid change, or circumstances outside your control have meant that responsibilities have been placed on you that you have neither sought nor expected.

To develop the right frame of mind you need an internal rationale about why you are there. Such a rationale provides the basis on which you can feel confident in your approach. Your rationale might be based on a positive decision to be in the role because of opportunities it afforded you. Or the internal rationale might be an acceptance that handling rapid change is now part of a job, even though this level of change was not anticipated when you took on the assignment.

It is well worth standing back, being explicit with yourself about why you are in a particular role and deciding the frame of mind you want to bring in addressing the responsibilities placed upon you. Knowing what will give you confidence and encouragement in carrying out these responsibilities is key to your feeling and believing you are making a worthwhile contribution.

Alex was an operations manager in a hospital. She was taken by surprise when a decision was made to merge two departments, with her being asked to lead the transition arrangements. Initially, Alex felt a mixture of reactions, including resentment and apprehension. She was disappointed that much of what she had previously been working on was going to be subsumed into a bigger operation. She felt anxious about whether she would be able to cope with uncertainties created by the planned reorganisation. Alex recognised that it was crucial was that she developed a positive frame of mind. She needed to move on from the initial resentment in order to bring a positive approach. She worked hard to understand the rationale for the change. She developed an internal narrative about the opportunities afforded by the reorganisation. As she talked through this rationale with others she became convinced that there were considerable merits in the reorganisation plan. At that point her confidence level in leading the change took a step upwards.

## In practice

- Be honest about your current frame of mind in leading or handling rapid change.

- Think through your internal rationale for why you are in this particular role.

- Recognise the self-talk needed to get your confidence to a level that will enable you to address your anxieties.

- Share with others your rationale about why you are in the role.

# UNDERSTAND THE EXPECTATIONS OF OTHERS

UNDERSTANDING THE EXPECTATIONS OF others is key to focusing your contribution in the most targeted and effective way. It may include reconciling the different expectations of key interests.

## The idea

You will have your own presumptions about what is a good-quality outcome, but crucial to progress will be understanding the expectations of different interested parties. A key starting point is identifying the expectations of those who have initiated or are funding the project or activity. Why are they investing resources and what are the outcomes they are seeking to achieve? What are their expectations on both quality and timescale? What is the type of trade-off that is acceptable to them between quality and timescale?

The expectations may be obvious because they are articulated clearly in a specification or project document. But sometimes expectations can be assumed rather than specified: therein can lie the seeds of misunderstanding and wasted effort. When you think expectations are unclear, it must be right to press those who are providing finance and personnel resources to be more specific about expectations.

There may be a wide range of people with an interest who have expectations. You may recognise that these wider expectations will only be partially met. It is worth seeking to understand how strongly those expectations are felt and how they might be partially recognised rather than just ignored.

It is worth checking periodically that the expectations of key parties have not changed. They might have evolved because of wider circumstances without the changed expectations being fully communicated in an explicit way. It is worth checking from time to time that you have not been inadvertently left behind.

Alex had been asked to take on the lead of managing the transition of the two departments. Alex recognised that she needed to understand what were the expectations of the hospital senior management. There was a clear financial rationale for the merger that was likely to be readily accepted, but she sensed there would be a wide range of different expectations about how the merger would be accomplished and what the ultimate benefits would be.

Alex knew she had to invest time understanding the hopes and fears of different interest groups so that she could build up a clear picture about the pattern of expectations in the different affected groups. She recognised that she would need to bring people from different areas together in order to build a shared understanding about expectations, addressing both the ultimate outcomes and the transitional arrangements.

## In practice

- Be clear about the expectations of the leaders who have decided on the change that is required.

- Push back if needed to get greater clarity on the expectations in terms of outcomes, quality and timescales.

- When you think the expectations are unrealistic, be willing to press for greater realism or more resources.

- Be willing to get key people in the room together to reach a greater mutual understanding about expectations.

# BE READY TO BE YOUR OWN BAROMETER OF PROGRESS

BECOMING YOUR OWN BAROMETER of progress will preserve you from the whims and prejudices of others.

## The idea

There may be a range of people around you expressing views on the rate of progress, or there might be a wall of silence with people keeping their views to themselves or ignoring the need for change. For some, the desire to reach a new steady state will mean that they want progress to take place unrealistically fast, and will be impatient with careful preparation and consultation. For others, their natural tendency will be to delay progress in order to retain as much of the present arrangement as possible. For some a sense of apprehension could mean a blanking out of the inevitability of change.

Understanding the emotions of others in either desiring or avoiding progress is key to bringing people along with you. For some you will be an advocate for greater patience. With others, your impatience may need to show in a deliberate and focused way.

Being your own barometer of progress will help preserve you from the whims and preferences of other people. If you see yourself as your own barometer of progress, this will enable you to weigh up the expectations and resource constraints that will allow you to assess a realistic timescale. The more objectivity you can bring, the easier it will be to assess the range of views you are hearing from others on progress. It is important that you are not overwhelmed by the diversity of views. What matters is that you have a clear rationale for what you think are appropriate next steps and a timetable that can realistically be applied to deliver those steps.

Alex was pleased that one group of staff were positive about the merger because they thought that equipment could be used more effectively. This group wanted the change to take place within days rather than weeks. Alex sought to affirm their enthusiasm, but needed to help them recognise that it would be a few weeks before a detailed plan covering all the aspects of the new department could be agreed and implemented. Alex acknowledged their enthusiasm while at the same time was clear about the rationale for the timetable.

With other groups Alex needed to be persistent in pointing out the merits of the reorganisation. She had to be deliberate in reinforcing the necessary timetable and not be put off by the apparent lack of enthusiasm.

Handling very different groups of staff reinforced for Alex the importance of being her own barometer of progress. She continually checked with herself that her assessment of what was doable over a period of weeks was both bold and realistic. She was not going to be diverted from this considered assessment by voices of doom or pleas for the new world to start immediately.

## In practice

- Recognise how people's emotional preferences will affect their assessment of progress.

- Be ready to bring measured patience—or deliberate impatience—in responding to the perspective of different groups.

- Be deliberate in being your own barometer of progress, having carefully weighed up the evidence.

# RECOGNISE AND ACCEPT THE RISKS

It is always worth being explicit about potential risks and knowing how to address them.

## The idea

I was recently part of a discussion about setting up a new Masters' degree programme in leadership. The relevant approvals had come through and the funding was now in place with a lot of enthusiasm to get the Masters' degree up and running as soon as possible. My approach was to focus on the risks without dampening the enthusiasm for the project. My aim was to ensure focused attention on potential derailers and uncertainties. For example, there would be the possibility of drop-out over a two-year cohort programme; but that was a risk that could be addressed by assessing the experience of other higher education institutions with similar programmes.

My intention was to focus on key risks and identify evidence from elsewhere about how significant those risks might be. Then we needed to identify what contingent steps were required to minimise the potential detrimental effects of such risks. The consequence of this focus on risks helped ensure an approach that was more grounded in realities.

Identifying say, the 10 key risks, and working through carefully how you assess those risks, is essential to developing a confident frame of mind in taking forward rapid change.

Alex recognised that she needed to bring a positive frame of mind if the merger of the two departments was to be successful, but she also knew that she needed to be very deliberate in recognising and accepting risks. She spent a couple of hours noting down what she thought were the top 10 risks and how they needed to be addressed. Alex then talked through these risks with a range of key players. She produced a chart assessing the significance of the risks and which steps were needed to address them. There were risks about, the disruption of day-to-day services, the cost being greater than originally anticipated, disaffection amongst staff and a potential reputational hit for the organisation. What mattered was keeping a cool head and ensuring there was an early warning of potential problems.

## In practice

- Keep looking at risks as a priority task and not an optional extra.

- Be honest in identifying and facing up to risks.

- Seek the perspective of others about the potential severity of risks and how best they are overcome.

- Draw on experiences from similar examples of change in order to understand the likelihood of risks and how to address them.

# ACCEPT THE INEVITABILITY OF SURPRISES AND SHOCKS

HOWEVER CAREFULLY YOU PLAN and manage risks there will be surprises and shocks. How you handle these unexpected events will define your leadership contribution.

## The idea

In any project there will be surprises and shocks. Others will be watching you to observe how you respond. Do you disappear or go into a state of denial? Do you go into a rant, blaming others, or do you sulk in the corner? How you respond to surprises and shocks will define how other people view your leadership contribution during times of rapid change.

Those around you will be looking for a calm and deliberate response. They will want to know that you recognise the implications of a surprise or shock and are able to bring an honest assessment of consequences. They will want to be reassured that you can adjust your perspective and are not going to be destabilised by the unexpected.

The greater your mental readiness for dealing with surprises or shocks, the better equipped you will be. Handling rapid change is exhausting enough without the emotional deflation that can come with an unexpected surprise. Hence it is important to know how you emotionally handle surprises and how you frame them into a wider context.

Alex was surprised when one of her key supporters resigned. Initially Alex wondered whether this was a reaction to the way she had been leading the project, but it was soon clear that there were domestic reasons for the resignation. Knowing that she had not been the cause of the resignation reassured Alex. However, there was a shock when Alex's boss showed her an e-mail of complaint from a different member of staff. Alex was disappointed to see this critical note. But she had assessed as one of the risks potential criticism from some individuals, so this type of complaint was not unexpected. She was emotionally prepared for this sort of response, even though she felt uncomfortable when she read the e-mail.

## In practice

- Remember how you have handled surprises and shocks in the past.

- When a surprise or shock happens, seek to understand your emotional reaction and not be overwhelmed by it.

- Accept that it is better for shocks or surprises to happen sooner rather than later.

- Talk through with trusted others how you keep calm when shocked or surprised.

# SECTION B
# THRIVING THROUGH CHANGE

# BUILD ON SUCCESSES

**6**

CELEBRATING SUCCESSES REINFORCES A positive frame of mind and builds momentum.

## The idea

Walls are constructed one brick at a time. The bricklayers may mark reaching a particular height of bricks with a well-earned break. Progress is made one step at a time as we put plans in place and build a coalition of supporters, ensuring that a particular change is introduced successfully.

As we recognise and build on successes we are reinforcing our own confidence and the confidence of the wider team. Marking a success includes celebration, even if this is just for a few moments.

Building on success is about recognising what is working well and how that understanding can be built into the next steps. A project that is going well should incorporate a process of continuous learning so that you and your colleagues are thriving through the expectations placed on you.

Alex was initially resistant to leading a major change programme. She needed encouragement and evidence of progress. When the plan began to come together and others accepted the approach she was taking, Alex began to grow in confidence. When Alex recognised that others had confidence in her, this awareness reinforced Alex's confidence in herself. She was recognising that she could thrive and not be exhausted by the change.

Alex was also conscious that she needed to keep up the morale and confidence of those around her. When the going got tough Alex knew that she had to keep affirming the progress that her colleagues were making. Alex was precise in the way she acknowledged the contribution of others and thereby reinforced the approaches and behaviours she particularly wanted to see in her colleagues.

## In practice

- See progress as a sequence of measurable steps.

- Mark reaching each step, allowing yourself and others time to celebrate progress.

- See success as learning from things that went both well or less well.

- Be precise in the way you recognise and affirm the progress that individuals have made.

- Ensure that the progress made as a result of the contribution of people junior to you is recognised by those in senior leadership roles.

# AVOID GETTING OVER-TIRED

In your enthusiasm your energy can seem unbounded, until you become exhausted.

## The idea

When we are very focused on leading or contributing to major change the adrenalin flows. We are thriving on the excitement of enabling change to happen. This sense of excitement keeps up our energy and resolve. We are thriving in a stimulating, if sometimes febrile, atmosphere.

We may then observe a colleague whose energy begins to flag. They appear to be foundering, whereas previously they had been thriving. If the pace of change is fast our sympathy for the colleague may be limited, but seeing a colleague become over-tired can be a warning sign that we are at risk of a similar response. In any team, if the pace of change is very quick there is a risk that team members will begin to be affected by exhaustion. When the pace of change is fast we need to know how to look after ourselves and our colleagues. Allowing ourselves to become over-tired can be hugely dangerous, both for the effectiveness of the shared endeavour and our own well-being.

Alex had been very impressed by the commitment of her deputy who had been adept in putting forward detailed plans, but at the start of one week the deputy became surprisingly indecisive. Alex recognised that her deputy had become over-tired and needed a break. Alex persuaded her to take a long weekend and she returned rejuvenated after a couple of days away. Alex took this experience as a warning sign that she needed to be looking after herself and protect herself from becoming exhausted.

Alex recognised that she should organise her time more effectively so she was not at everyone's beck and call all day. She needed to set aside time where she could be planning ahead. She needed to be more deliberate about when she left the office and ensure she did not spend every evening preoccupied about decisions for the following day. Alex recognised that there was a difference in how she needed to pace herself for a long-running project compared to one that had a deadline in two days' time.

## In practice

- Recognise in which situations your adrenalin flows so that your energy can seem boundless for a period.

- Be alert to what drains your energy most at busy times and limit the amount of time you spend on such activities.

- Think ahead and plan how you use your time and energy.

- Be deliberate in taking a break when you are in danger of becoming over-tired.

# 8 | MANAGE YOUR EMOTIONS

Our emotions are a source of great strength and also our prime liability. Managing them is crucial to being successful.

## The idea

Our emotions give us valuable data and early warning. When there is a touch of excitement we know that progress is possible. When we feel deflated we are conscious that there is a problem that needs to be addressed. When we have dialogue with another person we recognise that there is a prospect of purposeful engagement with a creative colleague. When there is frustration with an individual we recognise there is a risk of working to different agendas or on different timescales. It is always worth observing our mood and being aware what our emotions tell us about situations and people.

On the other hand our emotions can derail us. We may like someone a lot, which can mean we are not assessing what they say and do as objectively as we should. We may also have an aversion to another colleague, and therefore view their approach in a more negative way than is justifiable. We need to be able to raise an alarm bell in our head when there is a risk of an excessively positive or negative emotional reaction to an individual, affecting constructive progress and honest analysis of issues. Our emotions need to be both listened to and managed if they are going to be our biggest ally rather than a potential liability.

Alex recognised that she could have a negative emotional reaction to some situations and people. She knew she would not thrive if she let her emotional reactions overwhelm her.

Alex recognised that one of her staff annoyed her because of her tone of voice and tendency to criticise others. Towards the end of a day after a particular milestone had been reached Alex had an open conversation with this colleague about her reaction to other colleagues' approaches. This conversation was helpful but did not change the situation fundamentally. Alex knew that she would need to manage her emotional reaction to this individual, or else a strain in their relationship could develop that would be detrimental to the project.

## In practice

- Be deliberate in noting your emotional reactions to different people and situations.

- See your emotional reactions as providing you with valuable data while being wary about whether they are giving you misleading perspectives.

- Be willing to talk through your emotional reactions with individuals who generate unhelpful reactions within you.

# KNOW HOW YOU MANAGE STRESS

KEY TO THRIVING THROUGH change is knowing what causes you stress and how you manage your stress levels.

## The idea

Stress is often good. It keeps us alert and enables us to respond quickly in demanding situations. But stress over an extended period can be the source of debilitating strain. We need to be able to distinguish between good stress and bad stress. An element of competition can bring out the best in us. Too much focus on competition creates the risk of exhaustion and the stress of failure and disappointment.

There is the inevitable stress of schedules that need to be met and difficult conversations that need to be had. Handling rapid change will often mean that people's jobs disappear or are radically altered. In these situations stress is inevitable. What matters is how you manage the inevitable stress in yourself when making difficult decisions.

For most of us there is a pattern about what causes us stress. The early warning is often in our sleep patterns, or in our ability to concentrate on key activities, or the blanking of certain activities because we want to avoid the stress they cause.

Having a deliberate plan about how you are going to manage your stress levels during a demanding period is key to thriving through change. This is not about avoiding stress—this is about knowing how best to channel it, keep it to a minimum and take corrective action if it becomes expressed in damaging behaviour.

Alex knew that a danger sign for her was when she kept having the same conversation in her head about how to handle a particular situation. When she began to go round and round in circles she knew that she was getting over-stressed about a particular issue. In those circumstances she needed to write down what the issue was, the reasons why she was finding it difficult to deal with, and the next steps she needed to take. Once she had codified these factors she recognised that she needed to timetable how she addressed the issue in order to minimise the stress such an issue caused her.

## In practice

- Recognise what is good stress and how that enables you to be innovative and productive.

- Be explicit in identifying what will cause you stress and how best you will manage that stress.

- Be aware of the danger signs in you for when stress is about to become difficult.

- Recognise how best you manage the risk of stress in your team so the team continues to thrive through change.

# 10  KEEP YOUR PERSONAL ENERGY RECHARGED

Knowing how to keep your personal energy levels recharged is key to thriving through change.

## The idea

Your energy levels will vary depending on your health and well-being, your engagement in your work, your rapport with your colleagues and the sense that you are making a difference in your contribution at work. Keeping your personal energy recharged is both about how you engage in the work environment and the activities you are involved in outside work. Your personal energy in the work environment can be recharged through good-quality dialogue with colleagues, or the stimulus of your work, or the creativity needed in taking forward projects. Your personal energy outside work will be related to your engagement with family and friends and the wider range of activities you are involved in.

In handling rapid change, keeping your personal energy levels recharged will be key to maintaining momentum and resilience. This may to involve carving out time in the working environment to engage with those people who give you energy and resolve. Outside of work, maintaining your personal energy will require deliberate planning. This includes the way you engage with other people and being selective about the type of intellectual, emotional, physical and spiritual activities you are involved in. Keeping fresh involves mental stimulus, emotional support and a sense of making a contribution that matters in terms of family or community life. It is also likely to involve some physical activity that enables you to keep your body and mind alert. Physical energy may not be related to age: I am conscious that I have more energy aged 68 years than I had 20 years earlier.

Alex recognised the situations when her personal energy levels began to dip in the work environment. At such points she needed either a 10-minute break when she could turn her brain off, or a conversation for five minutes with one or two people who encouraged her. These were the people who gave her energy through their cheerfulness and positive demeanour.

Alex also watched how she spent her time out of the office. She knew that she needed a combination of good conversations and periods of rest and reflection alongside some intense, physical activity. Playing tennis was a passion for Alex, which she was able to do for most of the year because she was a member of a club that had indoor courts. The delight of playing tennis was a huge tonic to Alex and took her mind off work pressures.

## In practice

- Keep a watchful eye on your energy levels and how they change during the week.

- Be deliberate in how you spend focused time with people at work who help raise your energy levels.

- Plan how you organise your time outside of work so that some of it is devoted to activities that will help raise your energy levels.

- Give priority to whatever activities help reinforce your physical, intellectual, emotional and spiritual well-being.

# SECTION C
# MANAGE THE FALL-OUT

## 11 | KNOW YOUR PRIORITIES

BEING CLEAR ABOUT YOUR priorities and continually redefining them is fundamental to success in managing change.

## The idea

When you are required to lead rapid change or play a key part in ensuring rapid change happens effectively, you need to be confident in knowing and updating your priorities. You may feel deluged with a range of expectations and priorities. There might be a sense of excitement or mild panic, which means you are having to address the fall-out from what a wide range of people think is important. Hence it is important to know your priorities, continually review them and focus on their delivery.

Understanding your priorities may require you to be clear about what it is only you can do and what particular value you bring. Your priorities may well be determined by those senior to you, but you will often have the scope to shape those priorities. There will be an opportunity to decide how you tackle those priorities and how you involve a range of different people in doing so.

There is a balance to be struck between focusing on your priorities and being alert to changes, which will mean that your priorities need to adjust over time. Engaging with a particular individual might have been a relatively low priority, but because of views they have expressed, you may conclude that they are a key person to influence. Asking the question, 'What is it only I can do?' could lead you to conclude that there are particular problems or interrelationships that you are uniquely placed to unblock.

Alex was determined to have an action plan in place and agreed that the merger of the two hospital departments would take place within six weeks. This intent did not change. She prioritised her time to contribute influencing different parts of the plan. Alex was relentless in monitoring who she needed to influence and where the blockages were developing. She knew that she had the authority to press senior people to agree the components necessary for the overall timetable to be delivered. She maintained this focus, prioritising her time on issues she was uniquely placed to unblock.

## In practice

- Be clear about your personal priorities in ensuring rapid change is implemented effectively.

- Recognise the balance of priorities between delivery outcomes and the commitment and motivation of individuals.

- Keep coming back to the question 'What is it I am uniquely qualified to do in this situation?'

- Be willing to adapt your priorities. Be sure to explain to others how and why you are adapting those priorities.

# RECOGNISE YOUR IMPACT ON OTHERS

Your impact on others may not be what you expect; hence it is important to get feedback.

## The idea

People will respond in a variety of different ways to you—hence it is important not to assume that they will respond in the way you anticipate. Those affected by change will see this through their own personal lens. Their lens may be coloured by anticipation or apprehension and they may be looking for indications of what change might mean for them. This can easily mean they interpret what you say and do in ways that are particularly related to their situation. Your thoughtful expression might be interpreted as a gloomy prognosis about the future. When major changes are being introduced the demeanour of those leading the changes will quickly be interpreted in a far more specific way than ever intended.

It can be helpful to ask your colleagues what they most want from you: this can produce some surprising responses. Some may want guidance when you had expected them to want greater empowerment. Others might be requesting empowerment when you expected them to want clear direction.

Partway through any change programme it is worth asking those you are working with what they most appreciate about your contribution and what, going forward, are the main contributions they would welcome you making. The resulting open conversations can enable misunderstandings to be talked through so that you are in the best possible position to judge how to manage your impact on others.

Alex sensed that some of the people working for her needed more direct guidance than others, but she was experiencing push-back from others that implied she was too directive. She recognised that she was not taking into account that a couple of her staff had become increasingly capable in the last year and did not need the same level of guidance and support. Their push-back on Alex was about giving them more space because her current impact on them was limiting their effectiveness.

Alex also recognised that with some of the key partners she had been too deferential. She had grown up in a culture where clinicians were always held in the highest respect. Alex had been learning in recent weeks that unless she pushed hard she was in danger of being ignored by senior clinicians.

## In practice

- Ask colleagues you trust to give you feedback about your impact on key players both inside and outside the organisation.

- Use a variety of means of influencing others and be mindful about which approaches work best.

- Be open in seeking direct feedback from colleagues about your impact on them and be willing to adjust your approach in the light of that feedback.

- Recalibrate at regular intervals whether your impact on particular colleagues is going in the right direction or whether you need to change your approach.

# DON'T EXPECT TO BE LIKED OR THANKED

When handling rapid change you need to develop a thick skin, as you are unlikely to be liked or thanked by many of those directly affected.

## The idea

A judge in a courtroom knows that he or she will be thanked by one party, but is unlikely to be thanked by the losing party. When you are responsible for rapid change you need to develop a thicker skin, as you are unlikely to be openly valued by all those directly affected. Those whose jobs are at risk may see you as an ogre. To all those who face an uncertain future you will be an agent of doom and possible destruction. Some may see opportunities as a result of your actions and might even encourage you to be radical, but most are likely to keep their heads down.

Your bosses might thank you occasionally, but because of the weight of expectations on them they may forget to thank you as much as you would have liked. If the change for which you are responsible proves to be successful you may well receive accolades after the event. Even those who had feared a negative outcome for themselves might ultimately be grateful to you because the changes may have forced them to explore new horizons.

Most of us welcome the appreciation of others. When you are heavily involved in managing change you need to become less dependent on the approval of others.

Alex had enjoyed a good rapport and banter with her colleagues. However, the relationships became more strained because people recognised the authority and responsibility that Alex now carried. Alex recognised she had to distance herself from her colleagues in order to be objective—and be seen to be objective—in her judgement. She knew that this role involved delayed affirmation. The thanks would flow when there was a successful outcome, but would be withheld in the short term. Alex recognised that one of the benefits of this role would be to force her to become less dependent on the approval of other people. She knew she had to develop a thicker skin and that this job would enable her to do so.

## In practice

- Recognise the extent to which you are dependent on the approval of others.

- Accept that you will go through a period where affirmation is likely to be withheld.

- See this as a period when developing a thicker skin and being less in need of approval is in your interest.

- Do not allow limited appreciation from others to stop you from thanking others for their contribution.

# LEARN FROM WHAT DOES NOT WORK

MANAGING FALL-OUT INCLUDES LEARNING from what does not work.

## The idea

Not everything you do will work. Some of what you try to do will be ignored or backfire. Managing the fall-out involves differentiating between an adverse reaction when you are doing the right thing, and a negative reaction when the sceptics are right and you need to change your approach.

When there is a negative reaction it is important to seek to judge whether it is right to stick to your preferred approach or adapt your stance, acknowledging that you are learning from experience and taking people's views into account.

An important balance is needed between being resolute in pursuing your direction and being adaptable to take into account different and new perspectives. Others will bring greater and different experience and may well identify where you have not got it right.

If you continually widen your repertoire of approaches then you will be open to trying different things and be willing to withdraw and regroup when that is necessary. You may think that acknowledging when something is not working is a black mark on you. But people will be much more likely to follow you if they observe you being willing to learn from your experiences and being willing to adapt your approach in the light of new information and different insights.

Alex recognised that she did not have a lot of experience in building agreement about how to structure a new organisation. She had run projects before successfully and was drawing on that experience, but bringing two departments together was a new departure. Initially she was over hesitant, and then oscillated to become too prescriptive. Alex was learning all the time about when to set out a clear direction and when to engage with others and seek to define an agreed way forward.

Alex was heavily criticised by one group for putting forward a proposal that seemed to ignore their particular concerns. Alex thought they had overreacted, but acknowledged that there was some truth in their criticisms. Alex engaged with this group in a way which meant they addressed the issue as a shared concern rather than a two-sided disagreement. Alex won them round through her willingness to understand their perspectives and work more closely with them.

## In practice

- See apparent failures as valuable learning.

- Recognise that you are widening your repertoire of approaches all the time, learning through what is working well or less well.

- Be willing to acknowledge to others that you are continually learning and share that learning with others.

- When an approach does not work, try to work jointly to move forward rather than having a negative debate about what has gone wrong.

# HOLD YOUR NERVE

SOMETIMES YOU HAVE TO maintain a resolute approach and hold your nerve while those around you are uncertain or in disarray.

## The idea

It is right to keep listening and engaging. You want to be fully appraised of people's views and preferences. You want the best intelligence available about the potential implications of certain decisions and how people are reacting. You want to be willing to be adaptable in the way the case for change is presented. There may be new information, which means that some of the objectives and approaches need to change.

On the other hand, when you have thought through your approach and there is clarity about what needs to be delivered there is a moment when you hold your nerve and continue on the course you have set.

Sometimes the concerns and criticisms from one group of people may be matched by equally strongly held, but opposite, concerns from others. In those situations it is relatively easy to hold your nerve when you recognise you are on a pathway that bridges the divide between different groups with a genuine interest. What is more difficult is when you need to hold your nerve when you are in a minority. Holding your nerve can feel like a painful experience. It may ultimately be a cathartic experience, but there is a pain barrier you need to go through as you hold your nerve whilst others around you might be losing theirs.

Alex was concerned when a colleague who used to be her boss thought the approach that Alex was setting out was misconceived. Alex listened carefully to this person's perspective but did not think that her concerns were well founded. Alex recognised the points that her colleague was making and explained carefully why she was going to continue with her original proposals. Alex surprised herself in her willingness to hold her nerve in this situation. Alex had thought through the issue carefully and was convinced that her approach was the right one. A few months later her colleague acknowledged to Alex that she had been right to keep on track.

## In practice

- Hold in mind that sometimes it will be right to adapt your approach and on other occasions appropriate to hold your nerve.

- When you are inclined to be resolute think through why you are sticking to your approach and check that you are thinking through the effects of new data and different perspectives.

- When you think the right thing is not to change course, be clear about your rationale for doing so and be willing to share it openly with people who are taking a different perspective.

- Later in the process, be open to evaluating whether holding your nerve was the best course of action or whether in hindsight you might have handled the situation differently.

# SECTION D
# DRAW ON WISE COUNSEL

# SEEK OUT THOSE WITH EXPERIENCE

DRAWING FROM THE KNOWLEDGE of those who have experienced similar situations before will always provide valuable insights.

## The idea

Every situation is unique, but there are often parallels with the experience of other change programmes. The question is: how do you draw on parallel experience without being constrained by what has happened in other contexts? There is always the risk of following slavishly what has worked well in a previous situation without adapting it fully to the current situation.

When you seek out those with experience it is important to understand the context from which they speak and to be discriminating in how you interpret their experience. The story someone tells about his or her experience may have evolved into a convincing narrative, but it might not entirely accurately reflect what originally happened. Hindsight can be a wonderful thing in enabling a past event to be represented in more rosy terms than was the case.

A helpful approach is to be looking out for nuggets of insights when you hear stories of successful change programmes. Rather than just listening to someone's story, it can be helpful to ask some pointed questions such as: 'What were the three key lessons you learnt?' or 'What are the three main traps to avoid?'

Kim had been asked to lead a programme that was transferring responsibility for some areas of work from Europe to India. The intent was to reduce costs and maintain a similar level of quality. There was both excitement and apprehension about the move to India. Within Europe there was inevitably a concern about the transfer of work offshore and its implications for jobs, customer service and quality.

Kim sought out those who had led similar programmes in other parts of the business. He deliberately chose areas where the transition had gone both smoothly and where there had been major problems. He heard very different stories about what had worked well or less well. He was able to identify from these experiences both the preconditions for success and what were the main, potential blockages that needed to be overcome. Talking to a range of people was useful so that he was not captivated by the approach of one or two strong personalities.

## In practice

- Commit some time to seeking the perspective of those who have had similar responsibilities to you in the past.

- Be clear on the questions you want to ask so as to avoid having to listen to long stories where someone is justifying their own approach.

- Draw on a range of different perspectives to find key insights.

- List the key learnings from those with previous experience and periodically check back on how your experience compares to theirs.

# ASK NEUTRAL ADVISORS TO OBSERVE AND APPRAISE

NEUTRAL OBSERVERS CAN PROVIDE an independent view, as your perspective will be coloured by your own hopes or fears.

## The idea

When I was a Director General in the UK Government I would ask periodically for health checks of time-sensitive programmes. There was always a risk that leaders of such programmes would tell me what they thought I wanted to hear. It was important to me to hear an independent voice that would provide reassurance about whether progress was good or whether there were issues that needed to be addressed. Often an independent health check would pinpoint assumptions that needed to be re-evaluated or intended dangers that had not been previously fully exposed.

When I was engaged in major reform it was always helpful to have an independent person as a member of the steering group with a brief to observe and feedback on both opportunities and risks that were not being fully addressed. The neutral advisor could be someone from elsewhere in the organisation—an independent non-executive, a consultant or a specialist in doing health checks. What mattered was a choice of advisor who had relevant and wide experience, and who brought an independent viewpoint and the ability to assess clearly and calmly.

Kim decided that he wanted to draw on a range of neutral advisors. He drew on a consultant who had worked with previous, similar transformations in Kim's company and elsewhere. He invited this individual to sit in on some key meetings and provide feedback on both the evidence of progress and the attitudes and level of motivation of staff. A younger colleague had four weeks available between roles: she was commissioned to talk to a range of people to gain an up-to-date perspective of their experience of the transformation as it unfolded.

The transformation board included a couple of non-executive members from elsewhere in the organisation. Kim recognised that they were not entirely neutral as they brought perspectives from other parts of the firm; but they offered a wider perspective, which helped Kim appraise the relative success of the transformation programme.

## In practice

- See an independent perspective as essential and not an optional extra.

- Recognise that no one is entirely neutral. Everyone brings the perspective of their previous experience.

- Be clear on the brief you give a neutral advisor so they understand what you are asking of them.

- Do not become too dependent on the views of one advisor: ideally, always have at least two who are coming from complimentary perspectives.

# ENSURE FOCUSED COACHING CONVERSATIONS

Focused coaching conversations will enable you to think clearly about your next steps and develop coherent future plans.

## The idea

Good-quality coaching conversations provide a valuable way of focusing into your next steps and how they relate to your ultimate objectives. It is important to enter a coaching conversation knowing what you want to distil in that conversation. When a coach is skilled in asking the right questions they can help you clarify how recent experiences influence your approach to delivering longer-term objectives. The skilled coach can help you distinguish between what is fundamental and important, as against the perpetual noise that can interfere with building coherent, forward momentum.

It helps to enter a coaching conversation with clarity about the areas you want to explore and openness to new insights. There may well be a 'eureka' moment when you see how different perspectives link together or how a future direction is achievable. Good coaching questions allow you to draw insights together and end up with a new resolve, both intellectually and emotionally.

Agreement at the end of a coaching session about next steps, with these being written down by either you or the coach, provides a structure that ensures that a coaching conversation is not an indulgence that is quickly forgotten. Reviewing progress at a subsequent coaching conversation will help demonstrate how much has been embedded from the previous exchange.

Kim began a new phase of coaching when he took on this transformation project. Kim regarded the coaching sessions as an oasis of calm, where he could link together his intellectual and emotional reactions. Open-ended questions from the coach allowed him to explore his own narrative about what he was seeking to do and the progress he was making. The coaching allowed him to look at progress from a variety of different angles. In the first coaching conversation, he recognised that there were certain individuals who he was ignoring. In his coaching conversation he talked through what their perspective could be and decided how he needed to engage with them in order to understand if this assumption was accurate.

The coaching conversations helped Kim identify the relative importance of different priorities. At the end of the coaching conversations Kim was clearer about what he needed to bring to his next steps. He always left the coaching conversations with two or three new insights that would be key to making a success of the next period. The summary that his coach provided after each session was invaluable as a checklist that he would re-read periodically.

## In practice

- See coaching conversations as a priority and do not cancel them because of other pressures.

- Prepare carefully for coaching conversations, letting the coach know what you would like to cover and the type of outcomes you would like to reach.

- Use coaching conversations in a focused way to cover both your frame of mind and actions needed.

- Ensure that the outcomes of a coaching conversation are documented and periodically return to them.

# KNOW WHOSE JUDGEMENT TO TRUST

IT IS IMPORTANT TO be discriminating in deciding whose judgement you trust.

## The idea

When you occupy a key role in a transformation programme you will not be short of advice. Many people will want to offer their opinions. It is important to listen to views from a wide variety of people and consider their perspectives. You will want to be able to acknowledge the contribution of all those with an interest.

As you listen to people you will be assessing the significance of different perspectives. You might conclude that some people are looking at an issue from quite a narrow viewpoint: their perspective is valid but blinkered. You may observe that other people are able to see an issue from a variety of perspectives and can, therefore, bring a more balanced understanding.

You are likely to develop a perspective about whose views are particularly important and whose judgement you trust. You may think that someone's views are important, but you do not believe they offer a full perspective.

There may be other people you talk with who are able to give you a coherent explanation about future possibilities and implications. You may be convinced by their ability to see issues from different angles and begin to trust their judgement.

It can be a helpful technique to score out of 10 the level of trust you have in someone's judgement. This simple exercise can be used to identify three or four people whose judgement you trust most. They may become the people with whom you talk issues through in an open-ended way, knowing that you can trust their judgement and can have open conversations with them.

Kim was bombarded with views from a wide range of different people. However, there were three senior managers whose views Kim learnt to trust. He was able to have frank conversations with them in which they explored different possibilities and outcomes. Kim did not feel that these three were always seeking to push in a particular direction. They were able to provide insights about the consequences of different actions and the likely behaviours of different players. It was their insights about future responses that proved particularly useful for Kim. With these three individuals Kim could call them up for a five minute conversation, getting straight to the point about a particular issue and know that they would give him a quick, pertinent observation that would help him clarify the correct next steps.

## In practice

- Be explicit about whose judgement you trust and whose judgement you are more wary of.

- Develop a routine in how you consult those people you trust, including the use of short, focused conversations.

- Ensure you acknowledge the contribution of those people you particularly trust, and seek over time to make it a two-way mentoring exchange.

- Recognise that you may be seeking someone's judgement on a particular topic for a limited period. As you move on to a different role you are likely to be looking for new people with whom you can build similar, trusted relationships.

# KEEP TRIANGULATING DIFFERENT PERSPECTIVES

As a transformation programme unfolds it is important to be conscious of how different interests view progress.

## The idea

When I led a one-week programme recently at a higher education college in Vancouver, some of the students did not know what I meant by triangulating different perspectives when making decisions. One participant then gave a very clear description about the nautical use of triangulation in order to be clear where your vessel was located and was heading.

You may think you are heading in a particular direction that will enable you to reach your desired destination. Others might be observing rocks or reefs that are likely to impede your journey. You may be clear on what the overall desired outcome is. Others might use a similar range of language but have a rather different perspective on the desired outcome.

Triangulating different perspectives will involve asking key parties their views on the outcomes sought, progress made and potential blockages along the way. This enables you to test whether your perspective stands up to scrutiny and whether it has been understood in the way intended by others.

Triangulating different perspectives also relates to your personal contribution. You want to understand where others think you have had most impact and where they think you need to be contributing most. You may think that the contribution you need to make is in one direction; whereas when you talk to others they may think that the key contribution is different.

Kim was focused on getting the detail of the change management plan agreed. As he talked with various interest groups he received feedback that he needed to talk to key senior leaders in both India and Europe to seek to get them on-board. Kim was assuming their acquiescence meant agreement. Others with a key interest in the programme were adamant that Kim needed to build a greater sense of shared ownership of the programme at senior levels.

As the programme evolved Kim continually assessed his personal contribution with those who had a vested interest in the success of the programme. This triangulating process kept Kim alert as to how he should focus his personal contribution in the most effective way possible.

## In practice

- Be clear in setting out your approach and your next steps so that others know where you are coming from.

- Invite key other interests to set out their perspectives clearly as a programme develops so there can be open dialogue about different views.

- Always draw in a variety of perspectives so you are triangulating a range of viewpoints, rather than ending up with a dispute between two diverse perspectives.

# SECTION E
# KEEP LEARNING AND GROWING

# TAKE YOUR STRENGTHS TO THE NEXT LEVEL

WHATEVER YOUR STRENGTHS, YOU can always develop them further.

## The idea

We each bring strengths to our work. We may have been appointed to a particular role because others have recognised our capabilities. Our appointment might have been linked to an assessment about our potential for growing into a role. The best recruiters will often recruit on the basis of attitude and approach rather than skill. They recognise that what is key to success is an individual bringing the right level of motivation and attitude of mind that will mean that an individual can grow into a role effectively.

It is worth being clear when you begin a new role which strengths have been identified by those that appointed you. The more explicit this understanding the easier it is to focus on how you develop these strengths and potential, and assess the progress made. Others may recognise potential in you that you might not have fully appreciated in the past. From the way you interact with others they may see a potential in you to develop personal influence and impact skills that you had not appreciated were there.

As you work with a range of different people on a change programme, you may contribute in new ways. You may be pleasantly surprised by the type of contribution you can make. It is important to delight in the progress you see in yourself and keep building into your repertoire different ways of influencing others.

Kim had always been quietly spoken, contributing later rather than earlier in meetings. He had been appointed to this transformation role partly because of his skills in listening and influencing. Kim observed that now he was expected by others to contribute earlier in meetings than had been his previous practice. Gradually he became more willing to express his perspective at an earlier stage. He observed that people were listening to him and being influenced by him. Sometimes they would debate and disagree with the views he was expressing: Kim recognised that this was far better than having his views ignored by others.

Kim was encouraged by his boss to keep on this path of speaking earlier and more directly in meetings. Kim was grateful for this advice, which helped him reinforce his capability in influencing others. Kim continued to recognise that the bedrock for his capacity to influence others was that he could listen well and summarise effectively the perspectives that he was hearing.

## In practice

- Believe people when they identify your strengths.

- Acknowledge to yourself your strengths and do not be excessively modest about them.

- Allow your strengths to be deployed in new situations, taking one step at a time.

- And when people recognise potential in you, accept their observations and build on these latent qualities.

# TAKE STOCK ON A REGULAR BASIS

At the heart of the learning process is taking stock on a regular basis and continually reassessing your capabilities and aspirations.

## The idea

When you climb a mountain it is helpful to take stock about your progress from time to time. As you look back you see the progress you have made. As you look forward you observe the hill that is still to climb in the knowledge that you have already made a significant amount of worthwhile progress. When I walked the Machu Picchu Trail with members of my family we knew we had to stop on a regular basis in order to gather our energy. The steps upwards seemed endless, but each time we rested we were ready for the next one hundred steps.

On a long climb the physical exertion necessitates short breaks in order to mark progress and prepare for the next stretch. There is a risk in a busy role that we never take stock. We relentlessly stay focused on what is urgent; but it is only after we stop and take stock that we can gain perspective, and recognise the progress we have made. Taking stock on a regular basis involves calibrating what we have delivered and how we have made that progress. We may feel there is still a long way to go, but we may be surprised by the steps we have taken over a relatively short period of time.

It is important to bring a perspective that we never stop growing and learning. I am learning new approaches and ways of engaging and motivating people at 68 years of age. I will know that it is time to stop coaching and teaching when I cease to be excited by new learning.

Kim had become a 'feedback junkie' over the last couple of years. He kept asking people: 'What type of approaches should I be developing?' This openness to invite others to participate in his own development was endearing to many. This invitation did mean that Kim had to take seriously the perspective of others and be seen to test out approaches they recommended to him. Kim recognised that he needed to play back to people what he had experimented with and the extent to which he had built new approaches into his repertoire. Kim also recognised that not everyone's feedback was helpful. It was right to filter people's comments, recognising that often feedback said as much about the giver as it does about the recipient.

## In practice

- Be clinical in assessing what worked or did not work in the approaches you took to different situations.

- Set aside at regular intervals time to take stock about your learning and development, and share your reflections with a couple of trusted people.

- Avoid blaming yourself or others when your learning has been less than you had hoped: accept that there will be inevitable disappointments.

# KEEP TAKING STEP CHANGES IN YOUR CONFIDENCE

CAPABILITY AND CONFIDENCE GO hand in hand. We need a bedrock of capability and the confidence to believe in that capability.

## The idea

Our confidence grows as we see progress, but our confidence can be dented when we misread situations or people. Our confidence can be more fragile than others might anticipate. Recognising the roots of our confidence is important if we are to continue to build the momentum necessary for our own development.

It is helpful to understand the sources of your confidence, which may come from past experience, inner belief or the affirmation of others. We will know from previous experience what can dent our confidence and how best we handle situations where our confidence is low.

Sometimes we might describe our confidence in an outdated way and say we are unconfident in some situations, where current experience suggests that we are perfectly able to handle these situations effectively. Sometimes we need to update our self-description of the situations where we feel more or less confident. In situations where we feel less confident it can be helpful to deliberately put ourselves in that situation so that we are practising being effective in circumstances that had previously caused us discomfort. It is through experiencing those situations on a repeated basis that we can recalibrate our sense of where we feel more or less confident.

A degree of doubt is often useful to help us avoid becoming over-confident and falling into the trap of doing inadequate preparation.

Kim knew that he had to become more confident in dealing with senior people. He recognised that he had to use brief opportunities to get across his points clearly in an engaging way. He had to learn to do the 'elevator pitch' in a focused, clear and cheerful way. He understood that the emotional connectivity was just as important as intellectual engagement.

Senior people needed to feel that a conversation with Kim would be worthwhile, engaging and enjoyable. Hence Kim deliberately went out of his way to have short conversations with senior people, giving them information or insights that he thought they would find useful. In this way he developed an approach that he was increasingly comfortable with, which helped him build allies at senior levels.

## In practice

- Be up-to-date in your assessment of the situations where you feel confident or less confident.

- Deliberately put yourself in situations where you feel less confident, preparing your thoughts and words carefully as you enter those situations.

- Accept there may be a discontinuity between your appearance of confidence and your inner sense of your own confidence.

- Take careful note of feedback about when you come over as more or less confident, as this may not be consistent with your own self-perception.

# BE FOCUSED ON STEERING RATHER THAN ROWING

THERE IS OFTEN A temptation to spend time rowing when what is most important is thoughtful and decisive steering.

## The idea

A metaphor that rang true for a developing leader I was working with was the importance of steering rather than rowing. This insight helped shape the approach of that individual over the next few years: he subsequently became a Permanent Secretary and Head of a UK Government department. We may be very good at rowing and enjoy the physical and mental exertion which rowing entails, but what others most need from us is to steer a forward direction and ensure that the efforts they put into rowing produce worthwhile results.

With any change programme there are lots of detailed points to resolve, plans to prepare, calculations to be done and conversations to be had. We have excelled at doing the detail, which might be why we have been put into a leadership role, but the leadership role now requires a different and more strategic skill. We need to graduate from being a master of the detail to mastering the direction of a whole endeavour and being able to influence its direction and steer a considered course ahead.

Taking time to stand and reflect on the future direction may seem a lower priority than doing the transformation. Unless we stand back and see where a programme is going we cannot steer effectively through some of the inevitable shallows or storms.

Kim knew that he ought to keep a strong focus on forward planning. He kept being pushed down into the details by the demands of lots of different people. He recognised that the urgent was often driving out the important. Not far from his office was a small park with a bench that looked over a small valley. When Kim needed to get out of rowing mode he would go and sit on this bench and look over the valley. This view helped remind Kim to look beyond the immediate detail and see where the whole programme was going. He kept reminding himself that his prime task was to ensure the steering of the whole project. He had overall responsibility, but there were others who could carry out the detailed tasks.

## In practice

- Be honest with yourself about the pleasure you take in the detail and the rowing.

- Recognise when you are at your best in steering and bringing a more strategic direction.

- Encourage others to hold you to account and tell you if you are spending too much time rowing and not enough steering.

- Be deliberate in how you allocate your time. Set aside time for focusing on the important and not just the urgent.

# KEEP STRETCHING YOUR BOUNDARIES OF UNDERSTANDING

UNDERSTANDING AND APPRECIATING THE viewpoint of others is a never-ending endeavour.

## The idea

I spend a part of each year at Regent College in Vancouver, teaching one-week courses that involve leaders from all around the Pacific. I am always inspired by the range of perspectives of people from very different cultures. My boundaries of understanding are always being stretched by their different experiences, aspirations and interpretations.

It is always worth asking yourself, what would I think if I stood in someone else's shoes? This is particularly pertinent when you are working with someone from a different part of the world or with a contrasting cultural heritage and perspective. We can be more blinkered in our approach and understanding than we might realise. Seeking to understand where others are coming from is important within any organisation, where the assumption might be that there is a shared mindset.

Continually stretching the boundaries of our understanding is also about keeping as up-to-date as possible about the opportunities provided by new technology. Sometimes it is the recently retired who are the most adept at using information technology to best effect. They provide encouragement that the opportunity to gain new understanding is just as relevant to someone aged 70 as aged 20.

Kim recognised that he needed to keep stretching the boundaries of understanding in terms of how different European and Asian cultures addressed and responded to change in organisations. He recognised that there was likely to be a mismatch of understanding about the context and the use of language. He worked hard to understand how different approaches and phrases would be understood.

Kim sought to stretch the boundaries of his understanding by keeping up with technological change and the way markets were evolving. He also sought to understand more clearly how different ways of working were likely to be experienced by individuals and teams in different parts of the world. Kim was enjoying learning how different concepts were understood and how constructive behaviours were developed in different countries. At the end of the programme Kim looked back on his learning about cultural differences as the growth in understanding that gave him most satisfaction.

## In practice

- Be willing to stand in the shoes of others to fully appreciate their perspectives.

- Be excited in learning about the perspectives of individuals and groups who come from a different cultural background.

- Be deliberate in sharing your learning of the effects of people's cultural background on the way they work most effectively with others.

- Enjoy the prospect that you will be continually stretching your understanding about different people's approaches and behaviours for the rest of your life.

# SECTION F
# MANAGE YOUR CAPABILITIES

# STAY AGILE TO CHANGES IN CIRCUMSTANCES

THERE WILL INEVITABLY BE changes to the original intent or timescale that have to be accepted and not resented.

## The idea

There is a famous army phrase that, 'plans are worthless, but planning is everything'. There will always be changes in circumstances that will mean that your intentions are going to be continually changing. A plan is out-of-date a few hours after it has been written, but the process of planning will have generated clarity about constraints, possibilities and priorities. Engaging with a range of stakeholders will help to build a mutual understanding that ought to enable you to address shifting circumstances quickly and adapt intentions in a way which takes people with you rather than creates opponents.

When planning how you implement major change it is helpful to think through what approach you will apply to address changed circumstances. Some of the potential, changed circumstances can be identified in advance. Others will be unexpected. It is critical to acknowledge that there will be measured discussion about the response to changed circumstances.

A good athlete adapts to shifting circumstances. They will respond to changing weather conditions and to the decisions of fellow competitors. When leading elements of a change programme you are inevitably dealing with individuals whose behaviour can be unpredictable. You might have nurtured a particular relationship, but events outside your control may mean that the particular interlocutor's priorities change and their willingness to cooperate becomes more constrained. Keeping agile requires you to balance clarity about the outcome you are seeking to achieve with the need to reach accommodation with key people.

Kim had expected that the India arm of the business would be accepting about the timescale for implementation. But financial returns elsewhere in the business in India were less than expected, which meant they wanted the switching of work from Europe to India to happen more quickly. Kim initially resented this changed request because it had not been part of the original plan. But he understood the reasoning for this changed requirement and saw ways of partially speeding up the process. This was dependent upon him reaching agreement with those in the European businesses that the pace of change could be quicker than originally planned, if not fully at the speed sought by colleagues in India.

## In practice

- Even if plans have to change, keep focused on the importance of forward planning.

- When key parties use changes in circumstances as a reason for altering plans, examine the reasons carefully but be willing to be adaptable.

- See the need for agility as inevitable—but do not just be pushed around at the whim of different interested parties.

# KEEP INVESTING IN YOUR SKILLS

Updating and developing your technical and relational skills is a continuous process.

## The idea

We never stop needing to invest in our skills and capabilities. The speed of technological change is such that we can rapidly become out-of-date. Someone in your organisation needs to be at the cutting edge of information technology changes or else you can rapidly become out-of-date. Changes in legislation happen at a remarkably fast pace, requiring keeping up with the weight of regulatory requirements. The focus on financial propriety means that corners cannot be cut: hence the need to have access to sound legal and accountancy skills so that you and your organisation are above reproach.

Investing in skills is not just about technical competence. It involves understanding the implications of neuroscience and developments in psychology so that we understand human dynamics and the effect of new medical insights on decision-making and behaviours.

The best leaders are continually learning from others in parallel situations. They never believe that their way is the only way. They welcome engagement with others who are working in a similar dynamic world. The most vibrant learning often comes in work-shadowing experiences or in learning sets where individuals tackle shared problems and learn from each other's approaches.

Kim built a mutual mentoring relationship with two other people doing similar roles to him in other parts of the global organisation.

They met over Skype from time to time and talked frankly about the issues they were addressing. Kim went on a three-week development programme at a university business school, where he rubbed shoulders with leaders doing similar transformations to the one he was engaged on. Working on case studies and sharing strategies was powerful for Kim, both in terms of understanding techniques and in developing his approach to influencing key interests.

The dilemma for Kim was to ensure enough time was available for investing in his own development. What helped him to give this high priority was the acknowledgement that his effectiveness in any future role would depend on a combination of progress in his current job and evidence that he was developing his capabilities and leadership approach effectively.

## In practice

- Be deliberate in identifying people you can learn from and spend time with them.

- Develop two or three mutual mentoring relationships, ensuring that they are two-way.

- Be selective in the leadership immersion events you go to and always be clear how they have developed your skills and understanding.

- See developing your skills in human understanding and leadership as just as important as technical skills.

- Keep up-to-date with insights from neuroscience.

# MANAGE YOUR ANXIETY ABOUT YOUR LESS STRONG POINTS

WE CAN BECOME TOO preoccupied with the notion that our less strong points will mean that we are likely to be exposed as inadequate.

## The idea

It is inevitable that we worry about our less strong characteristics. For some of us the 'impostor syndrome' means that we have an underlying fear of being found out. This fear can be deep-seated and stem from home or school experiences. The reality is rarely as severe as the fear.

It must be right to be conscious of your less strong points, provided we acknowledge that there will be a range of ways in which they can be addressed. This might mean working closely with people who bring complementary skills to you. It could mean becoming gradually better at the aspects of your role that you feel least equipped for. It will certainly involve acknowledging that there will be some parts of your role that you will inevitably be better at than others.

It is important to develop an approach that either addresses your less strong points or manages them. What is unhelpful is being trapped in anxiety that flows from apprehension and fears. Anxiety at its extreme is debilitating and exhausting. There is a point when it is advisable to see a counsellor or a doctor. There are ways in which we can recognise and moderate our anxieties through routines that work well for us and through seeking to limit an anxiety from affecting other areas of our life.

Kim had a fear of being found out when he met with his boss. There was no substantive basis for this fear, as his boss was always supportive. Kim recognised that he needed to address this fear through effective preparation for meetings with his boss. Kim was careful in how he planned for these meetings, because he judged that if he could begin to control this anxiety with someone who was supportive, he would begin to equip himself to deal with future bosses who might be less supportive.

Kim recognised that he needed to train his brain to go into 'opportunity' rather than 'fear' mode, when there was the prospect of a focused business meeting with someone in senior leadership. Kim applied the mental image of putting this anxiety about engagement with senior figures into a box and then locking the box. One day he would be confident enough to mentally throw this box over the edge of a steep cliff, but not yet.

## In practice

- Be objective about your less strong points, taking into account the views of others who may be more positive about what you regard as your less strong points.

- Be explicit about the anxieties that can overwhelm you.

- Develop a strategy for handling your less strong points that will influence who you recruit to your team, what activities you focus on and how much you develop skills in areas where you are less surefooted.

# BUILD A RANGE OF SKILLS AROUND YOU

NO ONE PERSON WILL ever have a monopoly of the skills needed to lead a change programme effectively.

## The idea

You may start off believing that you need to do every task that the change programme requires. You then recognise that your role is to build up the right group of individuals so that they mould into a team. You will be looking for a range of different technical skills alongside the motivation to operate effectively on a joint endeavour.

If your skills are primarily numerical and technical, you will want people around you who are able to communicate effectively. If your key skill is being able to summarise key points and being able to communicate persuasively and inspire others, you will want to ensure that there is a strong technical capability available to you so that the analysis is well-grounded and convincing.

Appointing people in your own image to senior posts is a recipe for disaster. If everyone thinks like you then the approach of your team is likely to be one-dimensional. Within your team you want people who are willing to engage with different perspectives and are able to draw the best out of all those engaged on this shared endeavour. You want differences to be debated openly, but with a constructive intent. You will need to set the tone to ensure that different viewpoints are respected, with a desire to reach an agreed way forward.

Kim recognised that he brought project management skills, but was less skilled in financial management. He ensured that a young accountant was part of his team. Kim gave this individual licence to be involved across the full range of work and the authority to be explicit about the need for financial discipline. Kim recognised the potential in this individual and sought to give him the same opportunity to grow into the role that Kim's boss had given him. Kim was regularly appreciative of the contribution of this accountant but was also deliberate in giving him feedback when Kim felt that his interventions were not as productive or adept as they might have been.

Kim encouraged people to bring to open forum issues on which there was disagreement. Kim adopted a constructive tone in expecting honest and constructive debate about these issues. Once a conclusion had been reached, there was an expectation that there would be consistency in taking forward those recommendations.

## In practice

- Be deliberate in appointing people whose views and experience are different to yours.

- Recognise the skills you do not have and ensure you appoint people with those skills into your team.

- Expect people to grow their capabilities, mirroring the way you are seeking to develop your capabilities.

- Expect shared behaviours, but encourage debate about different approaches.

# KNOW HOW TO KEEP RESOLUTE AND BE MODEST

BEING RESOLUTE AND MODEST go hand in hand: they are not opposites.

## The idea

The best of leaders combine being resolute and modest. They are resolute in focusing on the delivery of outcomes and drawing the best out of all those working with them as a shared endeavour. They are modest in terms of eliciting a contribution from a wide range of different people and acknowledging the importance of the contributions that others are making.

Being resolute is about clarity of intent, and having a set of well thought through objectives, a pattern of expectations and behaviours that are reasoned, communicated well and acknowledged. Being modest involves continuously learning from others, acknowledging the contribution from a wide variety of sources, learning from what has gone less well, and giving people a hearing and not demeaning opponents.

How best you combine being resolute and modest will depend on the company you keep and the voices you listen to. It involves building a partnership with those around you who help keep you realistic and modest. Your underlying values are critical so that power does not go to your head, while you embrace the responsibility and authority you have been given. There are choices to be made about how you combine being resolute and modest. You have the scope to balance the freedom you have been given as a leader with exercising those responsibilities in a resolute and modest way.

Kim recognised that success leading a transformation project involved him combining being resolute in driving through the change, and being modest in terms of how he listened and engaged with all those who had a view. He needed to be modest enough to recognise that he should draw on the expertise of a wide range of different people, but also resolute enough to understand that it was for him to make the key decisions for the programme to be successful. It was this need to balance being resolute and modest that forced him to mature as a leader in terms of hard decision-making, become increasingly comfortable in himself as a leader, and more adept at inspiring people through challenging times.

## In practice

- Recognise who balances being resolute and modest well.

- Be honest with yourself about the ways in which you need to become more resolute.

- Be clear how you are going to exercise modesty through listening and engaging well.

- Be ready to explain how you are balancing being resolute and modest in different situations.

# SECTION G
# EVOLVE YOUR NARRATIVE

# WHY AM I HERE?

It is worth regularly updating your rationale about why you are in a particular role and the changing expectations on you.

## The idea

In order to maintain your commitment and vitality it is important to recognise a continually evolving narrative about why you are in a role. When you took on a particular role you were likely to have been given a job description, or to have developed your own narrative when you applied for that position. If you had been successful in an interview you are likely to have personalised the description of why you wanted the role in a way that was convincing to others. A risk is that you convinced yourself with a narrative that may now be out of date, but you maintain this narrative now because it was successful then.

It can be revealing to respond spontaneously to a question from someone else about why you are in a particular role. If your instinctive response is about the opportunity it provides to make a difference, then your self-narrative is likely to be helpful in enabling you to approach tasks with energy and expectation. But your spontaneous response might be that the job pays the bills and keeps you occupied. This type of honest, downbeat response indicates that all is not well and that you should reevaluate the positive aspects of why you are in a particular role.

If you are part of handling rapid change you are inevitably balancing meeting the expectations of those in authority with being mindful about the implications of the change for you. The more you can see the positives in the proposed changes—ideally with potential opportunities for you as a consequence of the changes—then the more convincing you are likely to be in your narrative.

Alex recognised that she had to keep her self-narrative up-to-date regarding why she was leading the merger of the two hospital departments. She kept reminding herself and others about the benefits of the merger. She could see the value of the conversations she was having and the way she had been able to influence others. As a consequence of good feedback she was able to remind herself that she was making a difference, even when some of her proposals were being criticised. When she occasionally felt frustrated, Alex replayed in her mind various positive comments about her contribution. She kept up-to-date and affirming her narrative of why she was in the role.

## In practice

- Keep in mind why you were asked to do your current role.

- Keep your narrative up-to-date, building on the positive affirmation you receive.

- Be open with others in articulating what you think is the positive good that can come out of your contribution.

- Beware if your self-talk implies you are the victim of circumstances with little or no scope to make a constructive difference.

# 32 · WHAT AM I FOCUSED ON?

THE CONTINUOUS REEVALUATION OF your focus is central to being a successful leader of transformation.

## The idea

Two questions to keep asking yourself are: 'What am I focused on?' and 'What should I be focused on?' What you are focused on may be a legacy of your interpretation of past expectations. It might be as a result of a routine that you are comfortable with, or you are meeting the expectations of others rather than being deliberate in where you focus.

It can be very helpful to periodically address the question of the direction of your focus and not get bogged down in current concerns. Your focus is likely to include a mixture of short and long-term intentions. There will be some areas that need your immediate focus or else there will be hold-ups to the overall programme. If you are to lead transformation effectively there also needs to be a focus on the longer term and how potential opportunities or blockages are going to be addressed over the longer term.

What you focus on needs to take account of the expectations of those in overall authority. Your credibility will depend on your willingness to engage with what others think are the key areas of focus, and your being confident enough in your own authority and knowledge to be specific about where you need to focus and where you can make the biggest contribution.

Alex was surprised by the preoccupation of her colleagues with their own discrete areas. They seemed reluctant to see the bigger picture. This reinforced in Alex the importance of her keeping a focus on the overall intent of the reorganisation and the benefits that would flow if the reorganisation was set up in a sustainable way. Alex kept reiterating the fundamental features of the new structure and the benefits that would flow from their introduction.

Alex was relentless in reminding people of these benefits. At times there was a risk of her becoming irritated by what struck her as the small-minded, self-interest of some of her colleagues. Alex recognised that she needed to be patient and persistent choosing her moments to remind people of the long-term benefits. She kept coming back to the question, 'Where do I need to focus my interventions in order to keep up the momentum of the merger?'

## In practice

- Are the areas on which you are focused still the right ones?

- In what ways might you be more focused on longer-term opportunities and potential blockages?

- What are the areas of focus where you can make the biggest difference?

- Do your areas of focus meet the expectations both of those in key positions of authority and your own expectations about what good leadership means?

# 33 | HOW AM I BEHAVING?

---

YOUR BEHAVIOUR WILL BE far more influential than your words.

---

## The idea

Others may or may not listen to your words, but they will certainly be influenced by your behaviour. Others will automatically mirror your behaviour. If you are grumpy they are likely to respond in kind. If you are positive about opportunities they are more likely to be positive than would otherwise have been the case. Your demeanour and behaviour will be infectious, whether you like it or not.

The words you use are important. Careful repetition of messages will be key so people understand the constraints and steps that are needed. Words alone will not make the difference that is required if a change programme is to be implemented effectively.

It can be helpful before the start of a day to reflect on what sort of behaviours you are going to exhibit during that day. It might be that with some people you want to be very encouraging and optimistic. With others you may want to bring a tone of decisiveness. With some individuals you might want to be exhibiting a degree of unhappiness so that they recognise that a change in approach is needed.

You might enter a meeting recognising that there is a risk that you will show irritation. You need to decide whether you want that irritation to show or not. Irritation and anger that explodes is rarely useful, but showing some mild irritation can have a constructive effect. Ask yourself if the behaviours you are exhibiting are consistent with your values and with the delivery of the objectives of the change programmes you are involved in.

Kim was conscious that he was working with colleagues from a range of different cultural backgrounds. It was important that he understood how his approach was being interpreted in both India and Europe. Kim did not always fully appreciate how his requests were being interpreted and what was the right tone in which to express those requests. He learnt that it was important to check out whether he had got the tone right before taking forward particular actions. Kim increasingly recognised that what was fundamental to his credibility was demonstrating that he was listening carefully and always giving measured explanations about the steps he was taking.

## In practice

- Recognise the importance of the tone you set and the behaviours you demonstrate.

- Be clear about how you want people to understand your behaviours and then be deliberate in expressing those behaviours in the way you act and talk.

- Crosscheck with others whether your behaviours are being interpreted in the way you intend.

- Be deliberate about how you apply different behaviours in different contexts. Take into account the personalities and cultural backgrounds of the individuals you are communicating with.

# WHEN DO I REFLECT?

BE DELIBERATE IN CREATING time for reflection, both on your own and with trusted others.

## The idea

When you are part of a change process there is inevitably time pressure. The accepted wisdom is that reorganisation needs to be implemented quickly so that the benefits of transformation can be realised sooner rather than later, with any period of uncertainty kept to a minimum. You are inevitably going to feel that decisions are needed more quickly than you would ideally wish.

When the momentum is relentless we can become too single-minded for our own good and not reflect on whether we are doing the right things in the right way. Where the pace of change is fast and the expectations are high, the need for reflection becomes more rather than less important.

We each need to find a way of reflecting on what works for us as individuals. This reflection might involve intense physical activity or quiet meditation. It might be quiet times on our own, or reflective engagement with others. Reflection will involve standing back and allowing your mind and heart to interpret the day-to-day in a longer-term context.

Reflection might also involve processing issues subconsciously. You might deliberately want to reflect on whether a particular aspect of the change programme is correct. You might both do some thinking on a subject and say to a couple of trusted advisors that you would like to work through the pros and cons of next steps in a particular area.

Kim identified his 45-minute train commute to work and his periodic flights between Europe and India as good times to reflect. When he had a knotty, detailed issue that he needed to reflect on, he would plan to do so on the morning train ride, when he could quietly record key points. Kim's long flights to and from India allowed him time to work through some longer-term issues. Knowing that he could use these flights constructively meant that he would look forward to the opportunity they provided for reflection, rather than becoming depressed about the prospect of being stuck in a metal tube for an extended period of time.

## In practice

- Be aware of when you do your best-quality thinking and plan to use those times constructively.

- See periods of reflection as key to your success and not as an optional extra.

- Be deliberate in making time when you reflect alone and when you do so with trusted colleagues.

- See times of reflection as being about intellectual, emotional, physical and spiritual renewal.

- Accept that when work pressures are at their most severe that the need for reflection will be even more acute.

## 35 WHEN DO I ACT?

BEING INCREASINGLY DELIBERATE IN deciding when to act is a sign of being comfortable in yourself and in the leadership you bring.

## The idea

When you take on a change leadership role, your expectation is that action and changes will occur sooner rather than later. You know you will be assessed by the actions you take. You are likely to feel under a lot of pressure to act and to be seen to act decisively.

The right steps might be to listen and reflect rather than act. You might have been appointed to a role because you are seen as someone who likes to be at the centre of the action. What might be needed throughout a change programme is a careful balance between reflection and action. You want to develop a reputation for acting at the right time and in the right way, rather than being in perpetual motion, making a rapid sequence of decisions at every available opportunity.

Once you have established your credibility in a transformation role you can afford to evolve your own narrative in terms of how and when you take action. You may want to ensure you have a reputation for being decisive, but also one for listening carefully and weighing up evidence systematically. On the other hand, you want to have a reputation for being timely in the way you make decisions and not continually putting them off in the hope of getting better evidence. It can be helpful to plan ahead with the timing of decision-making and what type of evidence you will need in order to make decisions in a purposeful way.

Both Alex and Kim were conscious that their contribution was being observed carefully by their bosses, their peers and their staff. They were both in goldfish bowl environments, with some people offering support and others who were waiting for them to fail. They both recognised that what was absolutely central to their impact was judging when and how to act. They needed their decisions to be respected and responded to constructively by diverse groups of people. They knew that their actions would not always be welcomed. They needed to have a clear rationale for those actions.

They both experienced growing self-confidence in making decisions and taking action.

It was one step at a time: sometimes if felt like three steps forward followed by two steps backwards. But they both recognised that their confidence as leaders was going in the right direction, with the need to regularly update their own narrative about how best to balance reflection and action.

## In practice

- Be deliberate in deciding where you need to take action.

- Allow yourself to pause before you take action that may not be popular, but then take the necessary action confidently.

- Keep updating your own self-narrative to take account of the type of actions you feel increasingly comfortable taking.

- Whenever an action you have taken has worked well or less well, take time to reflect and learn.

## SECTION H
# FRAME OF MIND

# ENSURE COLLECTIVE OWNERSHIP AND PARTNERSHIP

WHEREVER POSSIBLE STRIVE FOR collective ownership and partnership, building this up incrementally.

## The idea

Leading others through transformation is both a privilege and a responsibility. It is a privilege because of the authority you carry. It is a responsibility because you are influencing the impact of the organisation, and the lives of individuals affected by and working for that organisation.

Bringing the right frame of mind is core to the progress you make. This frame of mind needs to recognise the authority that you carry and the responsibilities that you bear.

As far as possible, you want to build collective ownership and partnership. You may be faced with an array of sceptics and opponents, but there will always be some elements of shared interests that can be built upon. When these people are disinterested in the eventual outcome, the energy they are prepared to commit in criticism may dissipate. There will always be some sceptics who can be won over through rational argument or through a sense of shared endeavour. Key is getting to a point where you have a large enough support base to be able to cease to be influenced by a vociferous minority.

Kathy had been given responsibility for a change programme in an insurance company that required a one-third reduction in the number of staff. This decision flowed from a tougher insurance market and the need to automate many of the processes. Levels of morale were low following the announcement of recent financial figures and the commitment to a staff reduction. Kathy knew she needed to articulate a strong narrative about how the 'burning platform' necessitated major change. She met with representatives from the different interest groups and built as much agreement as possible about how the change programme was going to be managed and next steps communicated. There was an acceptance that firm action was needed. From some there was a willingness to work in partnership, while from others there was scepticism.

## In practice

- Recognise what is likely to be the frame of mind of sceptics and critics.

- Keep talking to all those involved so there is as much mutual understanding as possible.

- Seek to find areas of shared acceptance and understanding with sceptics and critics.

- Accept that collective ownership will take time to build up and may never be universal.

- Be affirming even when others are reluctant partners.

# UNDERSTAND HOPES AND FEARS AND BUILD RESILIENCE

Understanding hopes and fears is central to building up the resilience of an organisation to cope with change effectively.

## The idea

When major change is announced the natural reaction of some people is excitement, while for others their first reaction will be apprehension. Perhaps both reactions will be intermingled: the dominant reaction will depend on an individual's personality and their reading of the implications of the potential changes on them.

You will have your own hopes and fears in taking forward a change programme. It is helpful as a starting point to understand the hopes and fears of all those affected. Their reaction might be coloured by whether they think they will have a job in the new organisation. They may have fears about the quality of the work they will be doing and their prospect in terms of pay and advancement. Sometimes their expectations will be unrealistic. For some their hope is that the problem will go away, when they need to come to terms with the reality that change will happen. For others their fears are dominated by anticipating the worst possible outcome.

Hopes and fears need to be aired. As someone talks through their fears they may come to recognise that the outcome might not be quite as bad as they had first thought. Your task as a leader is to understand their hopes and fears and seek to put them in a wider context. In this way you are seeking to enable both individuals and an organisation to maintain as much resilience as possible against the background of uncertainty.

Kathy was at pains to emphasise that if the company had taken no action now, the possibility was that it would eventually have had to close down. A major restructuring and reduction in the number of staff was needed in order to have any realistic hope that the company could survive and thrive. Kathy sought to address the fears of her staff head on, but was clear that the main hope for the business was effective restructuring of roles. She sought to build an understanding of the need for change through a clear message that the future of the organisation depended on a realistic approach, with job losses inevitable. Kathy sought to mitigate the fears through describing the type of severance scheme, which would have financial attractions for some. She never dismissed people's fears, but she was deliberate in seeking to temper them with realism.

## In practice

- Understand how you manage your own hopes and fears as you lead others.

- Create situations where people can talk through their hopes and fears.

- Bring practical realism about next steps.

- Keep repeating your message, because it will not necessarily be heard the first time, or even the second.

- Watch out for gossip where fears get out of proportion.

- Keep coming back to realistic hopes for the future.

# 38

# THINK THROUGH THE CONSEQUENCES

WE CAN BE SO focused on achieving a set of targets that we fail to think through the consequences.

## The idea

History is littered with examples of major changes that have been launched without careful thought being given to the consequences. Political decisions often seem to be influenced by short-term political gain rather than the evaluation of long-term consequences.

A decision to initiate a major change programme may have been taken by people above your pay grade, but that does not absolve you of responsibility to be alert to consequences and to set them out clearly. Not all consequences are inevitable; hence part of your responsibility is to highlight steps that might be needed to fully understand the consequences and mitigate the least desirable outcomes.

As you lead others it is important to work through the consequences of decisions and actions made by your team, both in the short and longer term. A risk is that you focus on negative consequences, when there might be potentially positive consequences that can be identified. There may be opportunities about new learning and different types of roles or markets that can be developed.

The consequences flowing from your leadership need to be seen alongside the consequences of other parallel changes inside and outside your organisation. We live in a dynamic environment where the consequences of different sets of actions are bound to influence each other in ways that we might not readily predict. Hence it is important to ask what other kinds of change are likely to impact on your areas of responsibility.

Kathy thought hard about what would be the consequences for the design of jobs as a result of the change programme. She could see positive outcomes in terms of more interesting roles, provided people grasped the opportunity that information technology developments brought. Kathy was also conscious that the finance department was going through major change at the same time, meaning that two parallel change programmes needed to be thought through carefully. Kathy was conscious that there were changes in the regulatory environment which she needed someone in her organisation to monitor. They did not want to end up with new processes that would have to be changed after a short period of time because of the shift in regulatory environment.

Past experience had taught Kathy that an important motto was 'Always think through the consequences of your actions'. She was relentless in working with colleagues to thoroughly examine the consequences of interrelated changes coming from both inside and outside the organisation.

## In practice

- Learn from the mistakes of others who did not think through the consequences of their actions.

- Be relentless in asking people to be explicit about the consequences of the actions they are proposing.

- Always take a wider view of the combined effect of different intended initiatives and external expectations.

- Keep reviewing how accurate you have been in anticipating consequences and feed that learning back into how you approach your next steps.

# 39 ENABLE DIFFICULT ISSUES TO BE FACED UP TO

WHEN THINGS ARE GOING smoothly we may not want to face up to difficult issues, but it is essential to do so.

## The idea

When you lead others you need to be aware that difficult issues will occur and need to be confronted. If any job is worth doing or any change programme is going to deliver results, there are going to be difficult decisions that need to be addressed. It can be helpful to set out and agree how difficult issues are going to be faced up to before the programme begins. You will want to emphasise clear factual evidence, honest and measured articulation of views, and good listening and engagement with each other and the facts. Also maintain openness to explore different options and take hard decisions where that is necessary.

Sometimes there can be an emotional reaction that something is going to be difficult when, after close examination, there is only one realistic course of action that might have difficult consequences. On other occasions there might be a difficult choice between equally unpalatable options.

As you prepare others for the inevitability of facing difficult decisions, you can invite them to reflect on what they have learned from handling difficult decisions in the past and how they might apply that learning in the current context. Your role might involve being alongside people as they face difficult issues while encouraging them to take full responsibility. You are not there to take their burden onto your shoulders. You are there to provide morale support.

Kathy foresaw a number of difficult issues about processes and people. She wanted to build up an acceptance of the need for change and move towards making constructive change happen. She was preparing a way by collecting data and talking about the inevitability of difficult decisions. Once the momentum for the change programme had become irreversible, Kathy decided it was right to face into the necessary decisions about dispensing with some processes that would be redundant with the advent of new information management systems. Kathy also decided that the momentum for change was strong enough for her to highlight the criteria that would be used to select who would fill the senior management posts.

## In practice

- Be consistent in identifying the difficult issues that will need to be faced up to.

- Do not pretend that all will be straightforward and recognise the inevitability that there will be hard choices.

- Seek to enable others to face up to difficult issues, while providing support without taking away the responsibility that is rightly theirs.

- Establish a timetable about when you expect difficult issues to be resolved.

# 40 | BRING ROOTED OPTIMISM

Always bring an attitude of mind that is rooted in realism, forward-looking and positive in tone.

## The idea

Someone who is always optimistic can be regarded as superficial and shallow. Someone who is always pessimistic is shunned and dismissed as a perpetual discourager. As a leader there is an obligation to bring both realism and a positive approach.

Realism needs to be rooted in evidence both about the facts and perceptions. Gossip needs to be continually tested by evidence. The current fetish for instant, highly-charged emotional viewpoints is a recipe for dangerous group paranoia, when what is needed is calm assessment of evidence, and measured, constructive, forward thinking.

I have always been influenced by the focus of Christian thinking on the importance of hope and new life. For me, it is important to consider the opportunities for new life any situation opens up and what are the sources of hope that can generate new energy and motivation. I observe that the best of leaders are always able to see positive possibilities in virtually any situation, and have an eye on the light at the end of the tunnel when all around are filled with gloom and despondency.

Bringing rooted optimism is not about distorting reality or practising self-deception. It is about bringing a combination of rigorous analysis alongside a belief that there can always be positive benefits in any situation if you work through the difficult questions with measured and decisive thoughtfulness.

Kathy believed that the insurance industry needed to become more efficient and more responsive to the needs of customers. She thought that the company had a strong enough sense of moral purpose to reach a new equilibrium, which would be good for both customers and staff. She believed it was right to be relentlessly positive about the future,whilst facing up to the big issues that the organisation needed to address confidently. Kathy's optimism came partially from her own personality and partially from her experience of leaders who had led change effectively in the past. Kathy deliberately talked to her people about how best they balance realism and optimism. She wanted them to work out a personal approach that took full account of their personalities and the type of future opportunities there could be within the organisation going forward.

## In practice

- Be persistent in encouraging individuals and teams to look at evidence dispassionately.

- Look for signs of positive progress, but always describe them accurately without overselling or underselling.

- Encourage honest debate about realism and optimism.

- Believe there can be positives outcomes from virtually any situation.

# BALANCE VISION WITH FLEXIBILITY OF APPROACH

# BRING CLARITY ABOUT OUTCOMES

As a leader others will be looking to you to bring clarity about outcomes and the necessary progress to reach those outcomes.

## The idea

A project may start off with a clear overall outcome such as an increase in throughput, a reduction in costs or a significant increase in positive feedback scores. But a simple desired outcome will raise a sequence of questions about what are the more specific steps necessary to achieve the overall intent. You will want to be in a position where you can bring as much clarity as possible. Sometimes the clarity you can bring is dependent on decisions yet to be taken, and so not possible at an early stage. Your credibility depends partially on how specific you can be about outcomes, and the type of timetable you can give for when desired outcomes are likely to be clearer.

As leader, one of your tasks might be to press specific interests to be clearer about the intermediate outcomes that are important to them. You bring an awareness of the bigger picture and the interaction between different streams of work. In order to bring focus to the overall endeavour, you will want to have a clear picture about how the different individual outcomes fit together and know where uncertainty in one area is having negative repercussions elsewhere in the enterprise.

Kathy was conscious that although the overall outcome of returning the business to profitability was clear, there were lots of question marks about the outcomes needed to deliver that intent. A one-third reduction in staffing levels had been declared as the broad intent, but there were decisions to be made about where the reductions should take place and the timescale. Kathy recognised that bringing greater clarity about these components would provide a degree of certainty that would enable the affected staff to think ahead about their own futures. There was advice to be sought from the HR Department first; but Kathy recognised that she needed to be as clear as possible about timescales.

On the other hand, she did not want to rule out the scope to adapt the plans in the light of new information and decisions. It was likely that a number of people would be leaving anyway, which would affect the extent to which a severance scheme was needed.

## In practice

- Understand which of the declared outcomes are fixed points and which are guidelines.

- Seek to understand how important it is for different groups of people to know the intermediate outcomes.

- Be as explicit as possible about the timescale on which intermediate outcomes are likely to be defined.

- When an outcome cannot yet be defined, be explicit about the reasons for this.

# BE READY TO HANDLE THE STORMS

ANTICIPATE THAT THERE WILL be storms. Be ready, both practically and emotionally, to handle them.

## The idea

Part of the training for sailing a yacht in the open sea is to recognise an impending storm and be ready to handle it. Storms are a regular experience for sailors. They see storms as inevitable and manageable. In any worthwhile change programme there will be storms to face. Some you will be able to foresee from a significant distance. Other squalls will arrive unexpectedly, but which might well disappear as soon as they arise. Other storms might go on for an extended period and need to be handled with steady determination.

The crew of a yacht will have practised how they work together in a storm. They will have their distinctive roles and know how to maintain their resolve. They will have contingency plans for the worst eventualities and will know when they need to call for emergency help. There are parallels from handling storms that can feed across to change programmes. They require careful contingent planning, with predefined roles and responsibilities, clarity about who is in the lead on particular issues and the ability to work in cooperation with others.

The key requirement is to be open with your team about the importance of planning for storms and having a clear, thought-through plan. If a team can handle a minor storm well it will reinforce its confidence in handling future, more significant storms effectively.

After the initial shock of the announcement, Kathy knew that some members of the organisation would seek to generate a storm of protest about the planned changes. Kathy thought through with her immediate team how they would handle a vehement reaction from a small group. They had to communicate the message of change clearly, and how the maintenance of jobs was dependent on radical action. They prepared for the eventuality that some of the criticism would be emotionally charged and personal. They recognised that they needed to weather this storm of protest so that the reorganisation could then be taken forward in a measured way.

Kathy wanted the team to keep lines of communication open throughout the organisation. Kathy did not want the prospect of a storm of criticism to mean that the barricades were put up, with a reduction to people's willingness to listen to and support the new direction.

## In practice

- Recognise the inevitability of storms.

- Plan carefully for how your team will respond to an unexpected storm.

- Prepare for the inevitability of criticism and how you would respond to attacks that feel personal.

- Prepare people to hold their nerve, recognising that storms often abate as quickly as they arise.

# KNOW WHEN TO ADAPT YOUR APPROACH

THE EFFECTIVE TEAM IS able to adapt its approach quickly and seamlessly.

## The idea

A flock of birds can switch direction almost instantaneously. At migration time the flock seems to know where to roost and when to fly off together to a different climate. The well-rehearsed team will have prepared how they are going to respond to changing circumstances.

The cycling team will have developed routines about when they switch roles if one of their number is unable to keep up the pace. The cycling team adapts its approach in response to decisions by opposing teams. The way they adapt looks spontaneous, but the tactics will have been carefully rehearsed.

Adapting your approach is not a sign of weakness. It follows from a careful reading of new realities. If key influential players begin to switch their priorities, you cannot ignore what they are doing. It is a sign of strength to respond decisively and not a sign of weakness. You need to be clear that you are not being unnecessarily bullied into a change of approach. Much as you may not like having to change your approach, you might have to accept the facts of a new reality, which means your position is not as strong as you had originally thought.

When you feel that your approach needs to be adapted, how you do so is important. Making the switch begrudgingly will sap energy. If you can put the need for the switch in terms of living with a new reality in order to keep delivering the best possible outcomes, then you are more likely to continue to have the support of people who might otherwise have opposed you.

Kathy was known for being a single-minded leader. She built strong loyalty amongst her teams. She recognised that she could sometimes focus on the original course for too long. It was important that she kept alert to when she needed to change her approach and when she could continue to be single-minded. She recognised that she needed to go through consultation with senior members of her team before she adapted her approach in a significant way. It was important that she explained her reasoning meticulously. Kathy did not want people to lose confidence in her judgement and could see this was a danger in some situations.

## In practice

- Recognise how you normally balance being resolute with being adaptable.

- Be clear about the difference between being adaptable and being pushed around by the views of others.

- Ensure you are able to have good conversations with your people when you think there is a need for adaptability.

- Be open in listening to others who argue that you and the team should act in a more responsive and adaptable way.

- See the willingness to adapt as a sign of strength and not of weakness, provided the rationale for such adaptions is explored and explained carefully.

# 44 KNOW WHEN TO HOLD FAST

THERE ARE CRITICAL MOMENTS when keeping people focused on the right outcome is crucial.

## The idea

When a football team is facing a skilled opposition it has to defend with resolution and determination. The defenders need to work closely together to anticipate where the attackers are going to exploit space. Effective defenders are alert to dangers, quick in responding to changes in strategy and adept at moving quickly to close down unguarded space. The defender will be alert to where their colleagues are positioned and how best to work with a teammate to catch out an opponent.

There are many parallels when you are seeking to counter vociferous critics of a change programme. You need your team to be acting as one, with the shared objective of holding fast to the agreed direction and forward plan. You want your team to be resolute in working together and in identifying flaws in your opponent's arguments. There are moments for listening intently to critics. There are times when their accusations need to be countered boldly, with your team acting together to ensure that your critics do not get the upper hand.

On some occasions your role is to inspire your people to hold firm to an agreed course of action with a clear rationale. Your task will be to reiterate the rationale, to emphasise progress so far and to be clear on the necessary next steps.

Kathy had ensured that the views of the sceptics had been heard and considered. She had modified her approach in some respects, but the overall timetable now dictated that a firm announcement about next steps needed to be made. The range of views had been considered but the sequence of next steps were now clear to move the business forwards. This was the moment when Kathy needed to be unequivocal and determined and show the necessary doggedness. Her language was both firm and calm. The future direction was clear. She was convincing, with most people now being willing to follow.

## In practice

- Recognise that there will be moments when you need to be unequivocal about the direction of travel.

- Accept that there will be times when you feel under a lot of pressure from opponents: be ready to absorb the pressure and then combat it.

- Accept that there are moments when obstinacy is a strength.

- Be clear when you are willing to retreat what your final boundaries are.

## 45 MANAGE THE PACE

BE DELIBERATE IN MANAGING the pace of change; fast is not always good.

## The idea

The individual cyclist who leads the pack over an extended period is unlikely to be the winner. The cyclist who works closely with others to share the lead will conserve their energy so that they have the opportunity to challenge for the finishing line. The sprinter knows that success is all about fast pace over a short distance. The long-distance runner deploys their energy over an extended period, accepting that they will vary their pace depending on the actions of their competitors, the terrain over which they are running and the environmental conditions.

There are moments when a fast pace is crucial, such as when decisions have to be communicated to a wide range of people at the same time. Even then there needs to be a measured approach in how this is done: an overriding focus on speed can easily lead to accidents and oversights.

If a change programme is going to be sustained, careful attention to the pace is key. You want to ensure that all those with a stake in the delivery and the outcome recognise the importance of the timetable and understand why that timetable is in place. You may well want the pace to be faster than many people would prefer, but that pace needs to be credible if your wider team is to be fully engaged with, and committed to, the programme. Managing the pace is not an afterthought: it is key to successful delivery.

Kathy recognised that the Board was expecting implementation by a specified date. She was deliberate in setting out a step-by-step timetable that allowed for review points. There was a desire in some to move very quickly, because of the fear of falling behind on the timetable. Kathy recognised the danger of panic in the minds of some if they were not able to make instant progress. Kathy saw her role as calming people down and enabling them to see that there was time for the next steps to take place, with a clear logic about the sequential nature of reviews and decisions. Kathy drew on various sports analogies, showing her people when the pace needed to be measured and when the pace needed to be fast.

## In practice

- Recognise the natural preferences of your people to move quickly or slowly.

- Draw on analogies from sports to bring out when different pacing is appropriate.

- Be ready to address situations when people are at risk of moving excessively quickly with not enough thought about next steps.

- Be alert to when there is a risk of the necessary pace falling behind and be ready with an approach to counter that.

# KEEP AHEAD OF THE PROBLEM

# THINK AHEAD TO SEE OPPORTUNITIES

It is important to be looking forward for opportunities and ensure the team is not too bogged down in the day-to-day.

## The idea

When a football team is under attack the focus of the defenders is on stopping their opponents from scoring a goal. But the good defender is alert to the opportunities that might open up when the majority of the opposing players are in attacking positions. The astute defender, when they are able to win the ball in a tackle, may see lots of forward space for a successful counterattack. The most dramatic goals often result from counterattacking football, with defenders swiftly turning defence into attack.

There is often a preoccupation with the immediate, with a focus on solving problems on a day-to-day basis. Such resolution is always commendable, but is not sufficient. Human motivation over an extended period requires individuals and teams believing that there is an overriding purpose for their activity with future outcomes and opportunities.

It is clear from the experience of information technology companies that those who thrive are always addressing future opportunities and are relentless in pushing the boundaries about technical possibilities and their application.

Kathy was clear in her leadership that the rationale for the change programme was not just about the sustainability of the business. She sought to understand how the insurance business was developing.

Kathy wanted to form a clear narrative to share with her people about the type of opportunities that the business was seeking. Her intent was to outline a credible future direction for the business, with the leadership identifying and grasping opportunities. Kathy knew that if she could paint a positive picture about the future of the business, this would help build a clear resolve about why the drive for increased effectiveness was necessary.

## In practice

- Observe how other organisations have responded to threats by moving into new opportunities.

- Be willing to describe how your leadership of change will enable the whole organisation to respond more readily to future opportunities.

- Encourage those affected by the changes to think into future opportunities and how their current work can contribute to delivering those opportunities.

# ANTICIPATE PROBLEMS AND BE READY TO RESPOND QUICKLY

SOMETIMES POTENTIAL PROBLEMS NEED to be explored over time. On other occasions they need to be addressed quickly.

## The idea

A decisive action might be interpreted by some as a panicked response, with the difference between the two being in the eye of the beholder. The challenge of leadership through change is knowing when to take early action, even though some people might interpret your decisiveness as a hasty reaction.

You want your team to be anticipating problems but not be overwhelmed by them. You want them to have the capability to respond quickly and yet be equally capable of dissecting a potential problem over a period and reach a considered view.

With any change programme it is important to be thinking ahead about what subsequent problems could occur and how they might be addressed. Anticipating problems enables a team to think about how they will address those problems together and be equipped to respond in a constructive and decisive way.

Not all problems can be anticipated. Individual team members need the licence to be able to address problems as they arise. They need to know when they can act on their own judgement and when they need to consult others. There needs to be a structure that allows for potential problems to be considered by the right mix of key people. But there also needs to be the licence for individuals to respond quickly to problems as they occur, without their feeling fearful of retribution.

Kathy wanted to ensure that all those involved in planning and implementing the changes recognised that there would be issues that would need to be worked through. She did not want to describe them as problems, as this might set a negative tone about a future pathway. Kathy emphasised the inevitability that there would be issues that would have to be addressed. She encouraged her team leaders to think through which of those issues would need to be considered more widely because of their general application, and which of the issues could be dealt with by individual managers or teams.

Kathy's concern was to develop in the team leaders a positive way of addressing the inevitable issues that would arise. She wanted to develop in them an adeptness in deciding which issues needed to be considered corporately and which were clearly their individual responsibility. Linked to this was developing in her managers the assumption that when they identified an issue with wider significance, it was for the manager to suggest a way forward rather than dump the issue on others.

## In practice

- Encourage your people to anticipate problems and share potential solutions.

- Develop the capacity to differentiate when potential issues need a considered corporate response, or decisive individual action.

- Be supportive when people respond quickly for good reason, even when they are learning from apparent mistakes.

- Be deliberate in sharing your approach to anticipating problems and deciding when to respond quickly and when to react after a considered delay.

# BUILD DYNAMIC ALLIANCES

BE MINDFUL ABOUT DIFFERENT alliances that can be built, sometimes with unexpected parties.

## The idea

The cycling peloton will often include individuals from different teams. Whilst they are in the peloton they are in each other's slipstream and will share the lead. There will be a moment when one competitor will seek to break away, but for much of the race the cyclists are cooperating in alliance with each other. Rugby players may be on opposing sides one Saturday and members of the same international team the following weekend. An opponent has become their staunchest ally and in a few weeks may be their opponent again. Members of sports teams are continually creating new, dynamic alliances and then moving on to create a new partnership with different people.

Any team leader is concerned to building up alliances within a team and between teams. It is right to be alert to the preoccupations and self-interest of different individuals. But as leader, you want to ensure the best is brought out of both your people and those with an interest in the outcome of the change programme. You want to build a team spirit amongst all those involved in the programme, even though some people may only be connected in a temporary or partial way. You will also want to create a dynamic alliance with colleagues in other parts of the business and with clients who are directly affected by the reorganisation. Hence the value of a dynamic alliance involving other parties such as HR, finance, IT support and other support services.

Kathy recognised that for the restructuring to be successful she needed to build alliances across the organisation. She needed her immediate team to feel a strong sense of mutual support and engagement, but she also wanted to ensure a dynamic alliance with partners in finance, IT and HR. People in these areas needed to be equally committed to the success of the venture, and be willing to contribute their ideas and resources. Kathy committed time to build supporters and alliances in the wider company. She refused to be put off when brushed aside and was relentless in developing strong networks and praising people when they were constructive in their support.

## In practice

- Be deliberate in thinking through what type of alliances are going to be important for success.

- Invest time in building a strong team with an emphasis on mutual support.

- Commit time and energy to building alliances right across the organisation and with customer groups where that is appropriate.

- See the time and energy committed as a good, long-term investment.

# RAISE THE SIGHTS OF YOUR TEAM

KEEPING YOUR TEAM FOCUSED on the desired outcome helps ensure they do not get bogged down in the day-to-day.

## The idea

The sports coach is raising the sights of his team during a break about what is possible in the next part of the game. They are continually seeking to motivate and inspire so that the players are focused on a shared goal they can take pride in. The coach wants to lift the team beyond their exhaustion and pain into the exhilaration of a successful result.

Sometimes your team might need a pep talk full of inspirational and emotionally loaded language. On other occasions you will need to raise the sights of the team by being clear about the next steps, and the resources necessary to help deliver those steps. Highlighting progress and support from key people in leadership roles will help bolster resolve to reach the goal.

Raising the sights of your team might also involve helping them think about what the future state will be like. The more they can anticipate the benefits of the changes, the greater will be the desire to reach that outcome. Helping them to imagine a much improved situation will provide an impetus to keep moving in that direction, however exacting the next steps might be.

Raising the sights of your team is not about diminishing the importance of the day-to-day work they do. The urgent has to be done, but the immediate tasks will feel less daunting and debilitating if they are seen in the context of being key steps to reaching an ultimate goal.

Kathy was concerned that some of her team were rubbing along with each other rather than bringing the best out of each other. She wanted to raise the sights of her team so that they could see the prospect of the team being significantly more supportive and, therefore, effective. She got team members to think about the characteristics of effective teams they had been a part of in the past and what they could do to enable the current team to adopt some of those characteristics. Through this focus on reflective learning Kathy helped change their expectations of what a good team looked like going forward.

Kathy was deliberate in ensuring that team meetings were not dominated by day-to-day issues. She ensured that at every third meeting there was a discussion about the longer term: this gave her the opportunity to be deliberate in reinforcing the future vision and ensuring that team members had their sights set on the right goals.

## In practice

- Be willing to use inspirational language at chosen moments.

- Be deliberate in seeking to raise the sights of your team in how they can operate more effectively.

- Ensure the forward agendas include a visionary element so that the team never loses sight of its ultimate aspirations.

## 50 | DRAW ON EXTERNAL EXPERTISE

Effective teams combine internal and external expertise in a creative way.

## The idea

When a team is willing to grasp hold of a problem and say it is determined to solve it, this determination is to be commended. There is then a judgement about whether bringing in external support undermines the team or adds to its capabilities. It is often the correct judgement that an existing team can solve a problem without additional support. They may well have the expertise to be in the best possible place to move an issue forward constructively. But it is always worth assessing whether this confidence comes from a strong sense of independence or from a considered diagnosis of what is needed.

Most teams benefit from being refreshed from time to time with new members. This forces a team to examine how it is operating to ensure that the most effective contribution is drawn out of all of its members. A forward-looking team is alert to the expertise that it will need going forward and whether this is available from within the team or whether external expertise needs to be brought in, either in full membership or at key moments.

Just as the general practitioner draws on the expertise of medical consultants on a regular basis, a good team leader is sensitive to when they need to draw on specialists to help clarify next steps. Drawing on external consultants in a focused and time-limited way is a sign of adaptability and self-confidence, and not of weakness or hesitation.

Kathy saw great strength in her team members. There was a lot of enthusiasm and commitment, but a lack of project discipline. At an early stage she brought into the team an experienced project manager in order to ensure a clearer forward structure and effective interlinking to different parts of the organisation. Initially, some team members were sceptical about whether a project manager would involve unnecessary bureaucracy. Kathy was careful in explaining her rationale and very supportive of the project manager as he began to impose the necessary discipline within an increasingly complex piece of work.

Kathy recognised that a representative from finance needed to be embedded within her team so that the accounting implications were properly understood and integrated. Kathy saw a clear need to involve someone who understood the customer behaviour perspective. The company drew on a number of external advisors in this area and Kathy included one of them in the project team. Kathy ensured that the team meetings included adequate space for these new members to make their mark. Kathy played back to the team what she observed about the benefits of this external input. The team cohered surprisingly quickly, as the original members could see the benefits flowing from these new participants.

## In practice

- Be specific about the expertise that is needed to ensure success. Decide how much of this is available within the existing team.

- Be explicit about the type of external expertise you are bringing in and why.

- Be affirming when you see the positive effects of this external expertise in the way the team is working and making decisions.

# SECTION K
# LISTEN, COMMUNICATE AND ADAPT

# LISTEN IN ORDER TO UNDERSTAND

There are people who appear to listen and those who listen to understand.

## The idea

You can be trained to look as if you are listening. You may have been told that you need to keep good eye contact, nod periodically and summarize back some of what you have heard: but listening to understand is in a different league. Often politicians have trained themselves to look good at listening and summarizing what they have heard, but may not be listening to understand. Listening to understand differentiates those who seek to influence public opinion or opinion within organisations from those who want to browbeat others into submission.

Listening to understand is not straightforward. It assumes an attitude of mind whereby you accept there are truths to learn from others, with you being open to changing your perspective in the light of what you hear.

Bringing an approach of listening to understand can involve adopting a coaching style of questioning whereby you invite people to both set out their perspectives and to articulate what they think would be the consequences of different approaches. Inviting people to consider how others might react helps both them and you develop an understanding of the implications of what they are saying. Key to understanding well is getting to the root of someone's primary concern, and thinking through how that concern is best addressed in a constructive, forward-looking way.

Joe was responsible for leading a project to rationalise the use of premises in a government organisation. The intent was to reduce the number of offices, introduce hot-desking and encourage more home working. Joe was used to leading projects, but had not led this type of project before. He talked to people who had led similar projects in other organisations to understand what had been their approach and how they had overcome pitfalls and objections. Joe built up a clear picture of what would be possible and what would be difficult. He established a set of contacts that would be useful to him as he led the project.

As Joe built his team he sought to understand the contribution that each team member would bring. He listened to their stories about their career and the development they particularly wanted to gain from their role. Joe set out a careful plan, outlining how he was going to listen to the different groups affected in order to understand their preferences and concerns. He rapidly learnt that there was a varied set of views that he would need to take into account.

## In practice

- Embrace the characteristics of those who listen well.

- Always be willing to demonstrate you have listened through the way you summarize what people have said to you.

- Identify the capacity to listen and understand as a key characteristic of team members you appoint.

- Ensure that within your team there is an acceptance that listening to understand is key to working to a successful outcome.

# 52 KNOW AND RESPECT YOUR AUDIENCE

TIME SPENT GETTING TO know your audience is never wasted.

## The idea

When you are leading a transformation it is easy to fall into an 'us and them' situation. There is a danger that 'the others' become branded as critics and opponents. It is inevitable that the inner team will build up a factual knowledge that others don't have. Hence, others might appear poorly equipped and not up-to-date, when this is just a consequence of one team having looked at an issue in depth whilst others are preoccupied with their own priorities. Any team needs to regard potential audiences as worthy of knowing and being respected.

A good conductor of a brass band will be conscious of the watching audience. The conductor will be adapting their introductions to the different pieces to take account of the location of the concert and the mix of people within the audience. The football coach prepares their team to perform in front of very different crowds: some in the crowd will be critical, while even their home supporters will be fickle. The football coach has to accept the inevitability that crowd dynamics will sometimes add hugely to a team feeling supported, while disparaging remarks from a crowd can have a damaging effect on confidence.

Your audiences will not only be those with a grandstand view. All those affected by the programme you are leading will be part of your audience. How they respond will contribute to the relative success of your programme.

Joe saw three different audiences that he needed to know and respect. The first audience had the governance responsibility for the reputation of the whole organisation. The second audience comprised people working in the organisation whose jobs and working lives were going to be affected. The third audience consisted of customers whose lives would be affected by decisions on the future location and organisation of the staff.

Joe was systematic in deciding who he needed to talk to within each audience. He decided how best to take their views into account and play back to them the steps he was taking, while explaining why he was using those particular approaches. He wanted to ensure good quality, open dialogue with all of these interests. He sought to understand in a precise way where he could make the biggest difference for each audience in terms of the success of the overall programme.

## In practice

- Be explicit in defining who your audiences are, both internally and externally.

- Seek to build a relationship with key people in each audience at both a formal and informal level.

- Be clear about what you respect about the views of each audience.

- Develop your approach about how you are going to distinguish good points from special pleading for different audiences.

# USE A VARIETY OF COMMUNICATION APPROACHES

PEOPLE ABSORB INFORMATION THROUGH different channels and at different speeds, so it is important to use a full range of communication approaches.

## The idea

A characteristic of successful change programmes is the use of a full range of communication approaches deployed effectively. Some people only believe that change is going to happen if they read it in black and white. Other people need to hear directly from a respected leader before they recognise that change is inevitable. Some people need a closely argued case before they will be convinced. Others need to know the headlines and be reassured that the details have been thought through.

There is a risk of seeing communication as an optional extra when it is central to the successful development and implementation of any change programme. Communication needs to cover why, what, how and when. The constant repetition of key messages is often necessary for people to understand that change is for real. Working in tandem to create convincing visual, oral and written messaging is fundamental.

Each person involved in a change programme needs to understand their role in effective communication and how what they say and do is being interpreted by others. Effective feedback is important on which aspects of communication are working well and which are creating more problems than they are solving. There is a balance to be struck between a consistent form of communication that is trusted, and using a variety of approaches which catch people's attention.

Joe held open meetings with staff when he visited each of the offices that were going to be affected. He let people know in advance that he was coming so that they could think through the issues they wanted to raise. Joe listened carefully to what people said and was as explicit as possible about next steps. When an issue had not yet been decided, Joe was open about why that was the case.

Joe sent out periodic, written communications, as he knew that he could only be present in the different offices on an occasional basis. He kept the communications short. It was better for meetings to be short and often than occasional and long-winded. Joe set up a blog in which he shared different stories about the potential effects and benefits of moving to more flexible working arrangements.

## In practice

- Draw from best practice in terms of how change programmes have used different communication methods.

- Be deliberate in using a wide variety of communication approaches.

- When you visit sites that are likely to be significantly affected, use this as an opportunity to maximise face-to-face communication.

- Keep getting feedback about which forms of communication are working most effectively.

- Be willing to quickly adapt your communication approaches in the light of feedback.

# RECOGNISE THE POWER OF INSTANT COMMUNICATION

INSTANT COMMUNICATION IS A factor of modern life. We have to seek to use it constructively.

## The idea

We live in a world of instant communication. We welcome the opportunity to send short messages of encouragement to people. Quick messaging is ideal for making or changing meeting arrangements. Short messaging also means that views are often expressed quickly and emotively without setting out the rationale for such views.

Instant communication can generate discontent or anger at a remarkably fast rate. It means that more heat than light can be generated quickly in a way that blocks constructive, measured dialogue.

Instant communication provides an opportunity to keep people informed about changes that are affecting them. When an adverse event happens, it does provide a means of reassuring people that plans are still on course. On the other hand, instant communication is a powerful tool for critics in generating a sense of annoyance.

It is important to be alert to how instant communication is likely to be used by critics and sceptics. Focusing your attention on those individuals who might be generating more heat than light is worth the effort. When instant communication has been used in a negatively way there is a judgement call about whether you respond in a way that counters the criticism or whether you allow for the instant negative reactions to die down. What is key is keeping an eye on which reactions generate momentum and which are regarded as the idiosyncratic views of individuals who are out of touch with what needs to happen.

Joe asked one of his trusted lieutenants to keep an eye on what was being said on social media about the planned restructuring. He asked for regular updates to be posted about progress on the organisation's intranet. This included period quotes from Joe about action taken and next steps. It became clear that in one office numerous emotive messages were being shared about the reorganisation that implied Joe's primary aim was to gain promotion and not to ensure constructive outcomes. Joe reiterated in his messaging the reasoning for the changes and why the outcomes would be better for staff in terms of more flexible working.

Joe recognised that one of the consequences of instant communication was that he had to live with criticism. The plus point was that the source of scepticism was abundantly clear, enabling him to respond before it gained too much momentum.

## In practice

- Seek to be on the front foot in the use of instant communication.

- Use instant communication judiciously: if you use it excessively it will be ignored.

- Accept that some people will use instant communication in a potentially destructive way: have a plan for how you counter such criticism.

- Ensure that within your team someone has responsibility for overseeing the use of instant communication. Monitor how others are employing it.

# KNOW WHEN IT IS YOUR MESSAGE TO GIVE

THERE ARE MOMENTS WHEN the words need to come from you and no one else.

## The idea

The individual who issues a new message every day is unlikely to be fully listened to after a period. If the message is too occasional, people will begin to wonder where you are and what you are doing. It is worth being clear about the type of messages you want expressed and when the instruction should come from others.

The starting point is understanding what people expect you as leader to be saying and doing. They will want the reassurance that you are clear on the future direction and that you have the confidence of key senior people whose backing is imperative for the programme to be implemented successfully.

When you are in a leadership role the expectation will be that you are setting the direction and tone. When the direction needs to be redefined they will be looking to you to clarify the new direction and why the changes have been made. When there has been disruption due to circumstances outside the control of the team, they will be looking to you for a reassuring message about the effects of this disruption.

You would want to build a pattern about who gives messages on particular topics. On operational matters you will want the individual responsible for operations to be in the lead in giving updating messages; but if there is a significant change of direction on an operational matter, you may want to be giving or endorsing that message. What is key is to keep asking yourself whether a particular message is significant enough to be given by you or whether it should be given by someone who has more day-to-day responsibility for a particular area.

When ministerial approval had been given for the reorganisation, Joe was clear that he needed to communicate the message that the plans were now to be implemented. When financial constraints meant that certain elements of the project were going to be delayed by 18 months, Joe recognised that the rationale for this delay needed to come from him. On lots of more detailed points Joe was clear that the messages needed to come from the head of operations in order to reinforce their importance. Joe wanted to keep his intervention in reserve on a number of operational issues. If there was some scepticism about the decisions announced by the head of operations, he wanted the freedom to come in with a short, clear message of endorsement for the changes.

## In practice

- Think into the minds of key clients and your staff about how they are likely to receive your messages.

- Delegate as far as you can messages on day-to-day issues.

- Recognise that the messages you give set an important tone for how people engage and take forward change.

- Be deliberate about the strategic level of your interventions.

- Watch out if you are over-doing or under-doing your messaging.

# KEEP IT SIMPLE AND CLEAR

CLARITY AND SIMPLICITY IS key to successful messaging on both major and minor issues.

## The idea

The advice, KISS (keep it simple stupid), needs to be ringing in our ears on a regular basis. We may be immersed in the detail and potential complications. We can foresee a range of different options and possibilities. There may be a myriad of risks we are addressing, but our messaging needs to be as clear and straightforward as possible. This is not about ignoring issues or complications. These have to be addressed and put into a wider context.

Our brain and heart can only take in a limited number of messages at the same time, so it is important to think through the first three key points that need to be made. If there are more than three points there will be diminishing returns. Your hearers may remember two or three points, but if you add numbers four and five, all your points they are likely to get lost in a mishmash of reactions.

Part of keeping it simple might be breaking down what you want to communicate into a number of phases, recognising that people can only absorb one phase at a time. A test of whether your messages are simple and clear is whether you can remember and articulate them without a detailed page of notes in front of you. You need to be as convincing as if you were in front of a television camera, maintaining good eye contact with the interviewer.

Regularly testing out what you want to say with trusted others can help ensure your messages are clear and simple. Responding to individual questions allows you to go into more detail on points of particular concern.

Joe recognised that his messaging needed to repeat clearly and unequivocally the rationale of the reorganisation and the key features of the timetable. When there was good news on progress he needed to link this visually with the future timetable to help people's understanding. Joe applied a maximum length of one page for any messages he sent out, which ensured they were more likely to be read. His insistence was that any message that he or his team issued should include a maximum of three points. Some found this discipline frustrating, but positive engagement scores from both staff and clients showed the benefit of sticking to a maximum of three points in any communication.

## In practice

- Set out standards about what you mean by clarity and simplicity.

- Be rigorous in limiting the length and the number of points within any communication.

- Ensure a consistency of approach and standards in communicators by other people in your organisation.

- Seek feedback on how messages land and when they are deemed to have been over complicated.

# BALANCE CONSISTENCY AND FRESHNESS

REPETITION IS ESSENTIAL, but new angles keep people curious and alert.

## The idea

When I worked as Principal Private Secretary for Kenneth Baker when he was Secretary of State for Education and Science in the late 1980s I came to greatly admire the balance he struck between a consistent, clear message and bringing in new, fresh examples. Kenneth Baker was leading major change in the education system in England. He had clear, unequivocal messages about the value of decisions being taken at a more local level within a defined national framework.

Kenneth Baker kept repeating the same messages in a way that listeners could understand. He kept using up-to-date illustrations about the problems with existing arrangements and potential benefits flowing from the reforms he was seeking to introduce. Journalists wanted to talk to Kenneth Baker because conversations with him were always engaging and included up-to-date evidence of progress within a consistent overall message.

In order to take people with you as you lead a change programme it is important to be clear about the consistent messages you want to be giving and how you keep those messages lively, fresh, up-to-date and relevant. Each month it is worth asking yourself what new evidence do you have or what new perspectives can you draw on which demonstrates the value of the course you are set on.

Joe had a coherent story about the benefits that would flow from a rationalisation of the offices and more flexible use of space. As he visited different organisations he kept building up new examples of how at different offices staff engagement levels had become higher because of the better use of space and more flexible working. He kept a log of these examples and deployed them in his written messaging and in his conversations with staff, especially with sceptics.

Joe recognised that what was important was not just the content of what he said but how he expressed it. It was vital that even though he was giving the same message again and again, it was imperative that it looked as if he believed in the messages just as much now as he had done a few months earlier. He needed to bring a tone of freshness and lively engagement to the enterprise, even when he might be feeling an element of frustration. Keeping both the context and tone fresh and consistent was important in maintaining forward momentum.

## In practice

- Be clear what are the consistent, unequivocal messages you need to keep repeating.

- Keep collecting evidence that you can use to keep the messaging fresh and relevant.

- Keep being curious about the implications of what you are taking forward so that you can examine it in a fresh way.

- Be mindful if you are in danger of getting bored with your own messaging and watch how you might come across to others in these circumstances.

# BUILD CONTINUOUS FEEDBACK INTO YOUR APPROACH

FEEDBACK IS A GIFT that should not be ignored or rejected.

## The idea

When we set out on a particular course of action we can feel that too much feedback is a distraction. But feedback is essential if we are going to respond effectively to what we are seeking to achieve. The sports player is going to get continual feedback from the decisions of their opponents, the views of their colleagues, the utterances of the coach, or the shouts from the crowd. The sports player has to operate with the sounds of continuous, vocal and divergent feedback bursting into their ears.

The risk for a manager is that they are oblivious to feedback. There might be mutterings and even plotting, but staff may be quiet and appear respectful. The complete absence of feedback is even more damaging that a welter of noisy, inconsistent feedback.

Being systematic in how you obtain feedback is helpful. At the end of key meetings you might suggest that there is a five-minute feedback conversation in which people comment about what has worked well or less well. After key presentations on the way forward, you will want to ensure you get feedback from key people about how your approach was received. For any programme it is helpful to have periodic, systematic feedback so it is clear how people are responding to the content and tone of your message. This will help identify problems that might not previously have been recognised.

Joe ensured that at all meetings with groups of staff there were people present who gave him honest feedback about what he said and how it was received. He ensured that the regular staff engagement survey provided useful data about whether staff felt positive or otherwise about the direction of change in the organisation. Joe was systematic in asking for feedback from a wide range of individuals about both the programme and his leadership of it.

When Joe received feedback he ensured he spent time considering it and then working out his next steps. In engagement with different groups of staff he deliberately revisited the feedback he had received and examined how he was responding to that feedback. When feedback was critical he sought to respond in a constructive way. Sometimes this meant being clearer that a particular course of action was necessary and unavoidable. When he was able to respond by changing the plan in some way, he made it known that he was responding to feedback in a forward-looking way.

## In practice

- Welcome feedback and respond to it constructively.

- Recognise that feedback says as much about the giver of the feedback as about the recipient, so do not take feedback personally.

- Be articulate in demonstrating your rationale about a future direction when responding to feedback.

- Recognise that often the right response to feedback is not to change the direction of travel but to change the tone of the approach.

# KEEP PEOPLE'S ATTENTION AND ENGAGEMENT

Be deliberate in keeping people's attention and engagement, recognising the preferences of different groups.

## The idea

Some people will be preoccupied with their day job and will not want to spend too much time thinking about longer-term change. They will either be trusting others to do that effectively or will be blanking out impending changes because they do not want to face up to them or because they distract from getting on with the day job. You may be pleased that these individuals want to focus on the day job, but you will want to ensure that you have their full attention at key moments when there are decisions to be made.

Other people will be constantly seeking your attention. They will be pushing you for information on a regular basis about what is going to happen next. Their preoccupation with next steps may come from a genuine concern that the future arrangements are going to work effectively, or this might result from an anxiety that is bubbling away in them. You will want to find a way of reassuring them so that they are keeping a focus on the day job and not letting anxiety about the future detract from their effectiveness.

Also being aware of the group dynamics in particular sub groups will be important, so you are conscious about how best you build on their engagement levels and ensure their attention is forward- rather than backward-focused.

Joe was conscious that staff in one location wanted him to visit regularly, whereas staff in another location seemed remarkable quiet. Joe was unsure what this indicated. He scheduled an early visit to the site, which had been quiet, in order to understand whether there were concerns that were not being surfaced. He was conscious that at the site where there were frequent requests for him to visit there were some individuals who were deeply unhappy with the direction of travel and who were creating discontent and unease. Joe recognised that with staff at this location he needed to be direct and explicit about the benefits of the forthcoming changes and the impossibility of continuing with the existing dispersed, geographical arrangements.

## In practice

- Be mindful who is responding well to you and who appears to be excessively quiet.

- Think through what type of engagement is going to work most effectively with different groups of people.

- Be mindful when the views of influential individuals are sowing seeds of doubt. Be deliberate in how you engage with both the bulk of the staff on those sites and the particular individuals who are provoking unrest.

# SHOW MEASURED AND DELIBERATE EMOTION

YOUR EMOTIONAL BEHAVIOUR IS likely to be far more influential than spoken words, so it is important to be deliberate in how you express your emotions.

## The idea

Our emotional reactions are important sources of data for us. They can be our biggest asset, but also our greatest liability if we let our emotions effect too much how we engage with and treat others.

You will want to be authentic in your leadership approach, so that people will see you as human and humane. Showing emotion is part of your humanity. But showing excessive emotion can create a sense of distance, apprehension and even fear. Your staff, colleagues and clients will respond more warmly to you if they see openness and generosity as your characteristics. But if they see you as excessively light-hearted or angry, they may have some hesitations about your ability to lead them in demanding situations.

The most effective leaders recognise their own emotions, give themselves time to interpret those emotions and then draw on those emotions in the way they outline a way ahead and interact with different issues and individuals. Everyone wants some sort of approval from their leader; therefore, clear, warm and explicit affirmation about what you appreciate in people is rarely wasted.

Being deliberate in how you deploy your emotions when you are feeling frustrated, disappointed or cross is a measure of maturity in a leader. Often the best approach is to depersonalise the emotion so your frustration is about the lack of progress on an issue rather than about an individual. This enables someone to feel less threatened by your comments and more able to view next steps in a constructive way.

Joe felt increasingly annoyed that one group of staff seemed to be putting 'their heads in the sand' about the intending changes. Joe was frustrated: his first inclination was to tell this group bluntly that they needed to face up to reality. He decided that the most propitious way to approach this issue was to have an open session with them about the potential benefits of the changes and how those benefits might influence the way they worked together. Joe managed the discussion so that it was focused on potential progress and shared issues, rather than him being directly critical of the staff. As the discussion progressed Joe decided that he needed to be more direct, talking firmly about the inevitability of the changes. He let his emotion show by speaking firmly while continuing to be warm and engaged with his facial expressions and body language. He wanted to give this group direct messages, but in a way that was embracing rather than dismissive.

## In practice

- Recognise the importance of the data your emotions provide.

- Be on your guard about displaying emotions in a way that might be counter-productive.

- Recognise that there will be moments when you need to speak firmly and directly, with your body language showing that you mean business.

- Whenever you feel that your emotions might be overwhelming you, be ready to stand back and decide how you want to express points. Build an emotional rapport rather than dissonance.

# SECTION L
# BUILD SUPPORTERS

# KNOW WHO ARE YOUR CHAMPIONS

Be clear who your supporters are and keep them well informed.

## The idea

At dark moments you may feel alone, with the whole weight of responsibility for a change programme on your shoulders. At these times it is worth reminding yourself who are your supporters and champions. An individual or group will have appointed you to this role and will be committed to your success. Others will want a good outcome from the work you are leading and will want to support you through difficult periods.

You may have champions in unexpected places. Senior people in the organisation may have identified your talents and may be deeply committed to this piece of work. They may be backing you, without your knowing directly of their involvement and influence.

It can be useful to map out who you think are going to be your champions and supporters and then decide how much time you are going to commit to engaging with them. When you do this mapping, it is worth clarifying why they are likely to be your supporters. Is it because they strongly support the project you are working to deliver, or is it because of a more personal commitment to you?

Some of your supporters may be fickle, especially if they see some aspects of the programme not working well. When there are issues, it is important to have a clear narrative about what are your next steps. A long explanation of why something has happened may be important for the finance department, but your supporters will want to know you have spotted the issue and have formulated a coherent response.

Joe knew that he was strongly supported by his director who had appointed him to this post: he had an open relationship with his boss, and regularly talked through issues and next steps with him. Joe recognised he needed to keep his boss fully appraised of progress and discuss impending issues with him. He also knew that his overall director general (to whom the director reported) was a champion of his. She would not want to be involved in the detail, but Joe recognised that from time to time he needed to send her reassuring notes on progress made.

Joe wanted to keep the support of the relevant leaders in both finance and HR. He sought to ensure that the finance lead was not constantly on his back asking questions: he had negotiated a timetable aimed at keeping him informed. Joe knew he would need the support of his HR interlocutor at key moments to ensure that recruitment happened quickly, hence the importance of keeping her support.

## In practice

- Be deliberate in mapping out who are your supporters and champions. Have a plan for keeping them briefed.

- Be mindful when you might be at risk of losing some supporters if a number of things are going in the wrong direction.

- Recognise that some people will be your champion at a distance and only need occasional updating.

- Remember that keeping your champions adequately briefed about progress will be worth the investment at a future moment, when you may need something from them.

# KNOW HOW YOU INSPIRE PEOPLE

Be deliberate in choosing how you inspire different groups of people.

## The idea

How have you been inspired in the past? Has it been as a result of a careful articulation about future possibilities? Has it been because you have been engaged by someone's vision of the potential future? Might it have been because someone has described, in a convincing manner, a way of doing things or a type of interaction that you think has considerable attractions? It is worth considering whether the type of approach that inspired you will also inspire others, or whether it was specific to your situation.

With any group it is worth thinking through how they are likely to be inspired. Your answer will need to take account of individual personalities and the context. For someone who needs to be convinced about the detail first, they will need to hear a narrative demonstrating that all the key elements are being properly considered. For others the focus point needs to be a persuasive description of a future state that captures their imagination: then they will be willing to engage with that vision in a motivated and purposeful way.

It is easy to assume that you inspire people by talking at them. A better way of thinking about this is to invite people to think about what would inspire them and then be informed by their responses. Many people are more likely to be inspired if they have played a significant part in developing the way forward rather than just being told what to do.

Joe asked a group of motivated staff what would inspire them. Their response was that 'more of the same' was needed, with regular communication and a sharing of positive evidence about how the better use of information technology was enabling people to do their jobs more effectively.

Another group of staff said that they did not know what would inspire them. Joe reframed the question in terms of what would help them feel more positive about next steps. This group talked about their fears and hopes in a way that gave Joe clues about the language and examples he needed to use to encourage them to be more committed to the necessary changes. Joe regularly read books and articles about major change in order to extend his knowledge of how best to motivate and inspire different groups of people. He picked up many new tips and tried them out.

## In practice

- Keep observing who is inspiring you and why.

- Ask the open question about what would inspire and motivate your colleagues.

- Be deliberate in varying your approach in order to enable individuals and groups to work out how best they are going to be inspired going forward.

- See inspiration coming from capturing a greater sense of what is possible rather than resulting from empty phrases.

# RECOGNISE AND CONVINCE SCEPTICS

SCEPTICS CANNOT BE IGNORED. You need to engage with them and then be clear on your way forward.

## The idea

Sceptics are helpful. They ask good questions and ensure issues are brought to the surface and worked through. If there are no sceptics there is a risk that you will be sailing ill prepared into a storm. Sceptics need to be cultivated, understood and engaged with. Their views need to be properly explored in conversations that examine the issues and are not dominated by personalities.

There needs to be a degree of accommodation with sceptics. There needs to be an agreed way in which the views of sceptics are considered, with a way forward then decided upon. Where a sceptic is part of a team, there needs to be agreement about corporate responsibility, once a decision has been made. You may well want to bring sceptics inside the tent so that their views are fully aired and they then contribute to the solution going forward. Many sceptics would prefer to be outside the tent so that they can continue to express critical comments without any sense of responsibility.

Spending time with sceptics is always worthwhile in order to understand and work through their perspectives. But when the conversations become circular it is important to recognise when a line has to be drawn under a particular debate and firm action taken. You may agree to differ with some sceptics. What is very important is finding out if they can be helpful or whether they are going to be a constant source of aggravation.

Sometimes the right answer for some sceptics and the organisation is a parting of the ways. If someone is very uncomfortable with the direction of travel of an organisation, it is neither in their interest or the organisation's interest for them to continue in that role. But the departure of sceptics should never be a knee-jerk reaction dictated by a dislike of your authority being questioned.

Joe worked closely with three sceptics within his organisation. He devoted time to understand their concerns and worked carefully through the rationale with them. He encouraged them to visit other organisations where similar changes had happened. One became convinced that Joe's plans were appropriate and became a valued champion. A second accepted the rational and acquiesced in the approach, but was never going to become an advocate. A third individual felt increasingly uncomfortable and began to look for other jobs. Joe respected this person's qualities and was happy to write a positive reference for them, knowing that they would be more fulfilled elsewhere.

## In practice

- View sceptics as bringing valuable insights.

- Engage with sceptics in a way that enables them to feel they are contributing to finding solutions.

- See winning over sceptics as an important validation of your approach.

- Recognise that for some sceptics there will need to be a parting of the ways: see that as inevitable and not as a failure.

# 64 WORK WITH THOSE WHO ARE INFLUENTIAL

SEEK OUT THOSE WHO others listen to: remember that those who speak with the loudest voice are not necessarily those who are the most influential.

## The idea

When I was a senior civil servant it was important to be aware of who the Secretary of State would listen to. This was likely to include the Special Advisors who had the ear of the Secretary of State: it was imperative to have good, open and constructive relationships with these powerful and sometimes idiosyncratic individuals. The Parliamentary Private Secretary and the relevant Parliamentary Whip would also be influential, especially if the governing party had a small majority. They were also likely to be trusted external experts who the Secretary of State drew on for ideas.

Having the sort of relationship with these influential people whereby I was aware of their predilections and could have conversations with them at key moments enabled me, as the Principal Private Secretary, to give sound advice to other officials about the direction of the Secretary of State's thinking.

When you are leading a change programme you can feel vulnerable to the whims of influential people. It is helpful if you are close enough to them to receive early warning of their next new idea—hopefully early enough to be able to talk it through with them before they begin to run hard with it. There are likely to be influential voices on any oversight or governance body to which you are accountable. You will want to get to know these individuals rather than just treat them as faceless bureaucrats or unhelpful amateurs.

Those who speak loudly in meetings can often be countered because the debate is in full public view. What can be more difficult is when an individual seeks to influence behind the scenes in a way that can undermine the momentum of the project.

Joe recognised that there were a couple of trade union officials who were especially influential with staff at some locations. Joe invested time explaining the rationale for the planned changes to these two people, and recognised that they would be expected to express some criticism on behalf of their members. Joe was at pains to demonstrate that he wanted to ensure the best possible outcome for staff and that the flexible working arrangements met the needs of an increasing number of people. He sought the advice of the trade union officials about how best to communicate next steps. He was not seeking confrontation, although he recognised that over time he would need to express firm views on some issues.

## In practice

- Be systematic in listening to those people you regard as influential, but be conscious about the extent to which they could have a negative or positive effect on outcomes.

- Be willing to invest time in building good, open relationships with those people you regard as influential.

- When people you have invested time in use the information you have given them to counter your preferred view, restrain yourself from getting cross with them as this is likely to be counter-productive.

- Learn lessons about good practices from those who influence well.

# 65  BUILD A BANK OF GOODWILL

BUILDING UNDERSTANDING AND CREDIT with a range of potentially influential people is rarely wasted.

## The idea

Being a good corporate citizen is important for a number of reasons. Effective organisations have at their core people who believe in the corporate good rather than just their individual areas of responsibility. The stronger a contribution you make corporately, the more you will see the implications of potential decisions from a wider range of different perspectives. The more you are supportive of your colleagues, the more likely they are to be willing to support you in times of need.

Building a bank of goodwill is not about building indebtedness in others. You invest in others because the organisation's success depends on each member doing well. When you encourage, support or coach colleagues, you are investing in what is right for the whole organisation. It is not about looking after yourself.

But the consequence of investing time and energy in others is that there will be a bank of goodwill available for you to draw on at key moments. This is not an invitation for you to expect others to support you regardless of the merits of your case. It is about building up the type of goodwill whereby colleagues will give of their time to engage with you on next steps and be willing to give you the benefit of the doubt when decisions and timescales are finely balanced. There will be times in a change programme when you want people to acquiesce to a change that they are not comfortable with. The more you have built up a bank of goodwill, the greater is the likelihood that you will be given licence to proceed, because your colleagues respect the way you are implementing forward programmes.

Joe reviewed how he had spent his time at the end of each week. His rule of thumb was that he wanted to spend two to three hours each week directly in support of his colleagues, either talking things through or mentoring. He did this partially because he enjoyed this type of engagement and also because he could see benefits in the growth in confidence and effectiveness of his group. This included people elsewhere in the organisation, where the investment was long term. The message spread through the organisation that Joe was a good person to talk through issues with. This meant that respect for his judgement continued to grow right across the organisation.

The consequence of his growing reputation was that whenever he put a proposal for additional resources or more flexibility to the central department, he met a sympathetic response. He did not always get his own way, but he always got a good hearing.

## In practice

- Commit time to talk issues through with colleagues.

- Offer to mentor people handling challenging issues.

- Keep in touch with people who you have worked closely with in the past, as your paths may cross again.

- Recognise who you have built up goodwill with.

- Draw on that goodwill in a deliberate and measured way, ensuring that you are not taking advantage of people's liking and respect for you.

# LIVE YOUR VALUES

# 66 BUILD TRUST

TRUST TAKES A LONG time to build up, but can be lost quickly.

## The idea

When you are leading a major change programme you have to build up a strong sense of trust. You want to build trusting relationships between individuals who are supportive of the programme. The governance arrangements are key in terms of building belief that decisions will be taken in the light of the best possible evidence. Getting the right people in the room at the right time and ensuring open and honest conversation, is a key step in building trust. Good governance is not an optional element. It is an essential a part of building up a strong commitment to the success of a joint endeavour.

Trust takes time to build, as individuals listen to each other and recognise the rationale of each other's viewpoints. Trust grows as people work together and see progress being made following creative and productive engagement.

Trust can be lost as soon as one party feels let down by another. When timescales are not met or the promised piece of action never happens, trust is undermined. When views expressed in a meeting are disowned afterwards, trust can be quickly shattered.

If you think others might regard you as having broken trust, it is important to talk with them to enable them to understand why you took a particular action so that your motivation is clear.

Helen was leading a major information technology transformation programme. The benefits of the promised automation had been sold hard by the company she was working for. As the project lead, her reputation was on the line to deliver what the company had promised.

Helen knew there was a degree of scepticism from within the client organisation, and faced that scepticism head on. Helen trusted herself and her colleagues to deliver the programme. But she knew that success did not come through blind trust. She needed to keep satisfying herself that her colleagues were able to deliver to the schedule and quality they had committed to. There were moments when delivery of next steps seemed at risk. Helen focused her interventions, with an approach geared to maintaining trust between the client organisation, her colleagues and her staff. She knew that she would have to make some direct demands within her organisation if trust with the client organisation was to be maintained.

## In practice

- Quantify in your own mind what trust means within key relationships in terms of what is going to be delivered and how.

- If you think there is a risk of you and your organisation being viewed as untrustworthy, address that issue explicitly and quickly.

- Recognise that if you build and demonstrate trust on small issues then you will be trusted on bigger issues.

- Be mindful that trust can be lost very quickly when half-truths are told.

# DEFINE SHARED VALUES

---

WHEN THERE ARE SHARED values there is a greater likelihood of a constructive resolution.

---

## The idea

There is little that is more destructive than two groups feeling self-righteous about their points of view, hiding behind their barricades and refusing to talk to each other, other than by slogan and megaphone.

When I work with a team that is engaged in leading major change, I often ask them to identify the underlying values that characterize the way they work as a team and the way they interact with staff and clients. I invite them to consider whether others will recognise in their approach the type of values they espouse. Ideally, I would do some fieldwork with different interest groups, to establish how their underlying values are expressed and experienced.

A team leading change might inherit a set of values from the parent organisation. Those values may be a perfectly good touchstone against which the team can assess their approach and be assessed by others. Thought may need to be given to how those underlying values apply in the particular context of the change programme. The detail of the values may well be less important than the process of talking through what they are and how they can be applied and assessed.

It is important that there is a feedback loop whereby there can be an honest conversation about the extent to which the values have been applied and identify when problems have arisen from only partial application.

Helen was conscious that there was a lot of underlying unease in the organisation. There was little sense of shared endeavour or of shared values. She initiated a sequence of open conversations about what should be the values that underlay the work of the team. Some participants wanted to focus on the day job and thought that discussing values was an irrelevance. Others saw the significance of reaching agreement about values, as they were a touchstone for the way the organisation should be working in the future.

Over time there was a gradual acceptance that the way the organisation operated during a time of major change needed to be rooted in openness, evidence, honesty and good communication. They worked through the implications of these values and assessed whether relationships were matching up with these values. There was an acknowledgement that these were the right values and a cautious belief that they would make a difference. Over time, much would depend on what emphasis Helen put on living those values.

## In practice

- Be relentless in talking about the importance of shared values.

- Create time for values to be discussed and their implications considered.

- Be willing to be an advocate and upholder of values, even though that might be painful in some situations.

- Allow others to test you on the extent to which you have applied your values.

# STICK TO YOUR VALUES, WHATEVER THE PROVOCATION

The consistent application of values means holding firm to them when you are provoked.

## The idea

Having a set of agreed values provides a constructive basis for reviewing decisions and actions. Putting a set of values together through consultation and engagement with your team can be a lively and enjoying exercise.

Values are an invaluable touchstone when you and your team are considering how to approach next steps or a difficult issue. Almost inevitably there will be moments when your values are not fully appreciated by others inside or outside the organisation. You may have said to your team that after a busy week they can leave the office at 5 p.m. on Friday. But a key customer may think that you are not providing good customer service if your team is postponing delivering a service until Monday. Your team may have a strong focus on rigorous quality control and be facing pressure from the commercial department to increase productivity. You have to give careful thought as to how this intersects with valuing your people.

When your values are under pressure it can feel as if you are being provoked. A first step is to understand the concerns of those who you feel are provoking you. From their point of view they may think their approach is entirely consistent with the values of the organisation and the values you are espousing.

What is key is an honest, open conversation so that you demonstrate you understand the concerns and values of others, and how these values are impacting on your approach and decisions. When you feel provoked it is important to recognise your emotional reaction, before you either respond hastily, sulk or complain.

Helen felt under pressure from the finance department to cut corners. She wanted to ensure the best possible quality of service when the transformation programme was complete: this involved extensive consultation in advance to know what mattered most to clients. The finance department wanted her to move more quickly so their financial targets could be met. Helen kept up the dialogue and refused to be provoked by e-mails, which bordered on the aggressive. She kept focusing on the long-term benefits of her approach. She did not complain about the finance department, as they had a job to do. She maintained a consistent approach, rooted in the values of the organisation and focused on the long-term benefits of the work she was leading.

## In practice

- When your approach is being questioned, seek to understand why others see things differently.

- Keep explaining why the values are important, both for your work and for the organisation as a whole.

- Keep calm in talking with those people who are provoking you.

- Share evidence that demonstrates living the values has enabled you and your team to deliver what had not been thought possible.

# KNOW HOW YOU HANDLE ETHICALLY DIFFICULT ISSUES

IT IS WORTHWHILE THINKING through in advance how you will handle ethically difficult issues before they arise.

## The idea

Ethically difficult decisions can take many different forms. Your approach to change may mean that some people's jobs are either abolished or transformed: how best do you weigh up these alternatives? The economic situation might cause you to make drastic reductions with some advisors saying, 'If you leave the changes for six months there might be the prospect of an economic upturn.' You may be weighing up whether some individuals should stay in the organisation or be asked to move on: they may have high level, technical competence, but can be counter-productive and on occasion can appear unethical. In all of these situations there is a trade-off to be made. The ethical dimension may arise because you are balancing your attitude and actions in relation to individuals with financial and economic considerations.

Many potential issues can be anticipated in advance. The sooner you can think through the issues in a dispassionate way at an early stage, prior to the point where making a decision is imperative, the better.

There are inevitably situations that have to be dealt with in the moment: for example, a key member of your team whose contribution is crucial to the next stage might have lost their cool and behaved inappropriately. Do you address this behaviour instantly, ignore it or flag up that there will need to be a conversation when there can be a pause and a period of reflection? Key is seeking to understand why someone responded in an inappropriate way. The right approach will depend on the context and the individuals involved. But inappropriate behaviour does need to be addressed in a timely way, or resentments fester and inappropriate behaviour can become the norm.

Helen recognised that one of her key staff could appear intimidating. He was very good at setting timescales and keeping to them, but his approach could be interpreted as overbearing and dogmatic. Some of the younger female analysts were clever, but had not yet developed a thick skin in how they responded to a tough-minded manager. Helen recognised that there was a risk of bullying complaints if her manager did not adapt his approach. At the same time she did not want to lose the manager's focus and forcefulness. She wanted to encourage him to direct his energy in a more constructive way.

Helen had a frank conversation with the manager about how his approach could be interpreted. She talked with some of the younger analysts about how best they might work with the manager and learn from his experience while not being intimidated by his approach. His progress was limited: she knew she would need to keep a very careful eye on the behaviour of the manager.

## In practice

- Identify the ethically challenging issues you might face in your role.

- Talk through with one or two trusted others how you would handle such issues.

- Ensure that within any team there is a shared understanding about how such potentially difficult issues might be handled.

- After you have taken action, be willing to explain carefully what you did and why you did it.

# 70 RETAIN YOUR INTEGRITY, WHATEVER HAPPENS

KEEPING CALM AND RESOLUTE when handling the unexpected is a key part of retaining your integrity.

## The idea

Problems happen. Life is full of unexpected and unwanted surprises. We plan ahead carefully, but decisions by others can have a dramatic effect on what is possible. A key customer might change their mind. A sponsor might resign. The financials change because of decisions taken elsewhere in the organisation or by a competitor.

Retaining your integrity is about keeping consistency with the values that you personally regard as important. You are clear that honesty is essential, so when do you share some sensitive information? You have focused on openness, so when do you consult on a sensitive issue? You have been strongly supportive of your leader, so when do you express doubt to them about their approach and attitude?

Retaining your integrity is about being consistent with your values and about choosing your moment to express reservations, recognising when somebody is most likely to listen and be receptive to your concerns. Retaining your integrity is not about hiding away and standing apart from others, it is about being engaged in a constructive and productive way. It is rarely about grandstanding or shouting accusations from behind a barricade. Accusing your interlocutor of inappropriate behaviour or blackmail is a highly provocative act and only justifiable in the most extreme cases.

Helen recognised that the transformation programme she was leading would have long-term benefits for her company's operations directorate but would create short-term disturbance. The Head of Operations, Bill, was adamant that there should be no disruption in the short-term and continually emphasised this viewpoint. Helen knew that she had to choose her moment to explain carefully to Bill what was going to happen next, along with some of the implications. He became increasingly hostile, insisting that there must be no short-term disruption.

Helen regarded Bill's approach as unrealistic. He began to accuse her of not listening and being too concerned about the project and not the business. He got increasingly irritated. Helen recognised that there were other factors contributing to this reaction. She kept her cool, even though Bill's approach was blinkered, unhelpful and overly emotional. Helen was determined that her integrity was not going to be undermined by this behaviour. She kept listening to Bill and showing evidence of forward progress, and refused to be intimidated by his behaviour.

## In practice

- Identify the key elements of your integrity that characterise your leadership.

- Recognise where others may have different priorities to you and, as a consequence, see your integrity as a negative.

- Be clear where your red lines are in terms of how far you are prepared to be pushed and when you will say, 'enough is enough'.

- Always be willing to give an explanation of how your integrity has influenced your decisions.

# SECTION N
# BUILD CREDIBILITY

# 71 BUILD TEAM CREDIBILITY

THE SUCCESS OF A transformation project and its reputation depends on the effectiveness of the whole team.

## The idea

You may enter a project with a strong reputation. You may have loads of relevant experience, but the success of the venture will depend on the contribution of the whole team, and not on you alone. You will want to set a clear direction and ensure that you keep your team fully informed and motivated. If there are weak links in your team, your client may begin to doubt the effectiveness of the whole enterprise. If a link in a chain cracks the chain ceases to serve its purpose. When an enterprise needs to act quickly, a single weakness can have a devastating effect on morale.

As leader it is always worth investing the time to make good appointments to a team: when you have doubts about appointing an individual, it is usually far better to begin the recruitment again rather than appoint someone about whom you have reservations.

When the work of the team is in full flow, it is worth periodically reviewing which are the strong links and which are the weak links in the work chain. Where links are strong, it is important to keep affirming those strengths. Where the links are weak, it is in the team's interest to focus on what encouragement or development is needed to overcome this weakness. Sometimes weak links need to be changed or the strength of the whole team will be undermined.

Building team credibility can be improved by ensuring that team members understand each other well and work together effectively. This means investing in building the internal capability and motivation of the team and observing how that team interfaces with partners and clients. Reviewing how a team is perceived by different stakeholders will give insights about how you move the team forward and develop it in a constructive way.

Helen was deliberate in seeking the views of influential people within the wider organisation about the contribution that different members of her team were making. Sometimes she needed to consider these views with care, as feedback says as much about the individual giving the feedback as the recipient. She wanted to build a picture so as to understand the frustrations flowing from the way different team members operated. To what extent were these inevitable consequences of actions taken by her team members? Or were some team members not responding as adeptly as they could do?

## In practice

- When appointing a team, look for people who will enhance the overall team's credibility.

- Look at each link in the chain to assess where there might be weaknesses that could inhibit the strength of the whole team.

- Seek the perspective of trusted others to identify the strong and weak links in the chain.

- Be direct with encouragement. Also challenge where the credibility and reputation of the whole team is in danger of being detrimentally affected by the less effective contribution of some members.

# ESTABLISH THE FACTS BEHIND CHANGES IN ATTITUDES

ATTITUDES CAN CHANGE FOR apparently unpredictable reasons, so it is important to understand why.

## The idea

When you are involved in leading a change programme, attitudes can change remarkably quickly. You feel that someone has been a blocker to progress: all of a sudden their attitude changes and they become an ally and not a critic. On the other hand, someone who has seemed very amenable to the plans suddenly begins to raise objections in a robust and even hectoring way. The natural reaction is to respond emotionally to the emotional reactions of others. The rollercoaster of emotions can then seem to accelerate.

It is always worth reflecting dispassionately why attitudes are changing. It might mean that the careful groundwork you have put in to building the case for change has eventually persuaded a sceptic. It could be that supporters of the way forward have had a private word with a sceptic, persuading them of the merits of the proposals.

The more worrying situation is where someone has acquiesced in proposals or has been generally supportive and then later becomes a critic. It is worth seeking to find out the factors that have led to this change of perspective. There will always be some considerations that have led to such a change of heart. It might be that you have unwittingly upset the individual through how you have expressed a viewpoint. It could be that some other event has happened that has meant that the outcome of the project you are leading has become far more important to this individual.

It could be that an individual has spotted some longer-term implications of the change you are leading which you had not previously recognised. Rather than being cross with the new critic, it is worth seeking to find out what risks they have identified that need to be properly taken into account.

The deputy chief executive had always been a supporter of Helen. She felt that she had his tacit approval for the programme she was leading. But his face changed from a benign interest into a furrowed brow. He began to ask pointed questions. Helen normally had good answers to these questions, but was getting concerned that he appeared to be taking a rather critical perspective on the transformation programme.

Helen felt herself getting increasingly annoyed by his interventions. She decided that she needed to ask him in an open way what was now worrying him about the project. The Deputy CEO was perfectly happy to have a conversation in which he shared his experience of another IT transformation that had gone wrong and his growing concerns about whether the programme would fully deliver what the organisation needed. Helen and the Deputy CEO reviewed data on IT programmes that they had both been involved in: this dialogue began to provide the sort of reassurance that they both needed.

## In practice

- When attitudes change, recognise there will always be underlying reasons for that change.

- Seek to depersonalise discussion so it is about the issues and not dominated by emotions.

- Be curious about changes in attitude; believe that understanding those changes will give you new insights.

# DISSEMINATE THE EVIDENCE OF PROGRESS

Beware if the evidence of progress is only in your head.

## The idea

You may think that a lot of progress has been made, as may members of your inner team. In your mind's eye you knew what you wanted to achieve and you have reached that point. Two key questions are: is that progress real or illusionary, and has anyone else recognised the progress made?

We like to motivate ourselves by being clear about the progress we are making. Keeping up our motivation requires us to believe that we are making progress, but the test of realism is important: do others also believe that progress is being made? Asking hard questions about the evidence of progress is important, both to ensure a realistic assessment and to provide data to those who have an interest in progress.

Disseminating the evidence of progress in a convincing way depends on finding an approach and tone that means the recipients feel they are being treated as responsible and interested grownups. The dissemination of evidence of progress might, for some people, be a few headline facts that illustrate the approach is working well. For technical experts the evidence of progress will need to be data focused, with a recognition that their professionalism is being treated seriously.

Those who have an interest in the outcome of a transformation programme will want to be reassured on a regular basis that careful thought is being given to their concerns and that progress is being made.

Helen's team had a tight deadline to meet. Each member wanted to focus on their individual contributions. The initial reaction to requests to show evidence of progress seemed to distract from getting the job done. Helen had to be firm that collecting evidence of progress and sharing it was key to keeping wide support within the organisation. The team needed the goodwill of a wide range of stakeholders, and would need their support at key moments—hence Helen was meticulous in ensuring she sent out a fortnightly briefing note across the organisation that was short, factual and honest. Her notes were always carefully expressed in terms of the benefits that would flow from the transformation, even though some short-term disruption was inevitable.

## In practice

- Beware of falling into the trap of thinking that progress has been made when others don't share this view.

- Be rigorous in checking that the progress you think has been made is recognised by others.

- Be meticulous in disseminating evidence of progress in ways that will bring people with you across the organisation.

- Accept that repetition will be necessary.

# 74 DEAL WITH UNTRUTHS FIRMLY

UNTRUTHS CAN HAVE AN insidious effect, undermining credibility and shared endeavour.

## The idea

When someone says to you for the third time that they did not receive your e-mail or letter, you begin to wonder what might be going on. When someone keeps telling you that a project is going well but gives you no supporting evidence of progress, you might wonder whether progress is as good as you have been led to believe. When an individual highlights only positive pieces of evidence and does not draw attention to areas where progress has been slow, you may wonder whether they are offering an accurate account.

We can probably all remember occasions when we have felt under pressure to deliver and have wanted to put the best possible gloss on progress; but we may also remember occasions when not highlighting challenges has been unhelpful in the long term. We may want people to think everything is going well, but successful projects require absolute honesty in identifying both signs of progress as well as evidence that advances have been limited.

Particular risks come through part truths, or portraying the truth in a particular way. We may be persuaded, or want to be persuaded, by evidence that supports our preferred action or outcome. Asking 'How firm is the evidence?' helps bring us back to reality, if we and others want to be persuaded in a particular direction.

When an individual or stakeholder has blatantly told untruths, it may be either because they are deceiving themselves or from deliberate fabrication. When a serious deliberate fabrication is spotted, facing up to it head on is essential. When an individual has been untruthful or blatantly economical with the truth, their rapid exit from the team is probably inevitable. The bad apple has to be removed from the barrel quickly if the other apples are to stay fresh.

Helen became increasingly worried when one of her managers was persistently reassuring but could offer only limited evidence of progress. Helen recognised that he was under considerable pressure to deliver. She was clear with him that he needed to be absolutely honest about progress and the risks going forward. When an external review of his area took place the reviewer found major problems, with many questions unanswered. The manager was defensive when challenged by Helen and began to blame others for the problems. Helen required him to have a clear plan to address these problems within a week, or she would expect his resignation.

## In practice

- Be alert to when someone is not being entirely straight with you.

- When facts have been distorted, be robust in expecting an honest assessment of the evidence.

- Demonstrate that where there is untruth or obfuscation that you will address it head on.

# PREPARE CAREFULLY FOR DIFFICULT CONVERSATIONS

WE ARE OFTEN JUDGED by how we handle difficult conversations, so investment in preparation for them is never wasted.

## The idea

The risks when it comes to handling difficult conversations are either that we leave preparation until the last minute and we feel that we have to 'wing' the conversation, or we become excessively anxious and over-prepared.

Difficult conversations are a fact of life for any leader. Once you have had a number of difficult conversations, you recognise your probable emotional reaction and what is likely to work well or less well in such a conversation. Preparing for a difficult conversation includes having the right evidence and facts available to you, but you cannot predict every question you are going to be asked and be word-perfect for every possibility. Effective preparation is about being clear on the underlying facts, the key points you want to make, the likely reaction of the individuals involved in the conversation and the outcome you want to achieve.

When you know you are going to have a conversation that you and others are likely to find difficult, it is worth being deliberate in choosing the timing and location of that conversation. You might want to give advance notice that you want to talk about a particular subject. You might want to see a conversation as part of an on-going discussion. In the first conversation, you may want to set out your concerns; this will enable the other individuals to think through the implications of their perspectives before having a substantive, second conversation.

You might be having difficult conversations in parallel with both a client and your staff if there are differences of interpretation and expectations. At the right time you could talk with them together; but at first you might want to speak to them separately if there is a lack of alignment between key clients and your staff.

Your staff needs to know that you are willing to have difficult conversations both with them, clients, and others in the organisation. They also need to know that you will want to talk through the evidence before you are willing to have conversations that could lead to conflict or major disagreement.

Helen recognised that one of the directors in the organisation and one of her key staff were at odds with each other. Helen's member of staff had been abrupt and over sensitive. Helen was also conscious that the director could be very demanding and not listen to practical concerns. Helen needed to have a firm conversation with each of them, which she prepared for carefully. The director was grumpy but recognised the points that Helen was making. The member of staff was surly and resentful, feeling that she was not being fully supported by Helen. Helen needed to have a second conversation with this member of staff when she had thought about her perspective more. Helen kept a careful eye on progress, and knew that she might need to get the two of them together in the same room at some later point.

## In practice

- See difficult conversations as an inevitable part of your job.

- Allocate time to think through your approach to a difficult conversation and the key outcomes you want to achieve.

- Seek to understand how individuals are likely to react to what you are going to say.

- Maintain a focus on the best interests of the overall enterprise.

# SECTION O
# BUILD CAPABILITY

# CREATE AN ENVIRONMENT OF CONTINUOUS LEARNING

WHATEVER THE EXPERTISE WITHIN your team, creating an environment of continuous learning prompts people to keep fresh in their approach and be open to new ideas.

## The idea

When a team is working well, there is a risk that members think there is no more to learn. There is a risk of their being too reliant on the approach and expertise that has always worked, rather than being open and curious about new ideas and approaches. For those working on IT programmes the pace of change is so fast that the risk of complacency is less than in other disciplines; but even so, there can be a risk of relying on what you know well rather than adopting new and more efficient approaches.

The risk with specialists is they see learning as related principally to their specialism. They dismissed as 'soft skills' understanding more about how people react in different situations and what sort of team dynamics can facilitate the most productive outcome.

Creating a culture of continuous learning is part of the responsibility of any leader, equipping people for both current and future roles. The time commitment to personal and team development can easily slip away when the pressure to deliver to a specific timescale is strong. Scheduling individual and team development may be difficult, but should not be dropped if the leader wants to commit to continuous development of their team. For many people, motivation in the present flows from investment in their future as they continually refine their approach.

Helen was conscious that within her team there were professionals with long experience and younger people eager to learn. She set up mutual mentoring arrangements across the team, inviting the more experienced members to pass on their knowledge to the younger members. Helen brought in an experienced team coach to facilitate three-hour workshops with the team to help them embed their learning. This included examining what had gone well, as well as thinking through ways in which they could improve team effectiveness. Helen was relentless in asking team members what they had learnt over the past month and how they were going to apply that learning going forward. She shared how she had been learning from different groups through effective communication.

## In practice

- Be willing to share your own learning with those working with you on a periodic basis.

- Seek to pair up people who can learn from each other.

- Protect time for individual and team development and focus that time so that participants do not feel bored.

# BE DELIBERATE IN RECRUITING FOR ATTITUDE

IN THE LONG RUN, recruiting for attitude trumps recruiting on the basis of past experience.

## The idea

Most of us have known organisations where the attitude is downbeat. Changes and new ideas are unwelcome. There are memories of a glorious past, which become ever more rose-tinted as time passes. New recruits absorb this negative attitude quickly and soon get sucked in to the malaise.

Recruiting for attitude is about looking for individuals who have both the aptitude and will to learn. They may not have lots of experience or qualifications of the highest level, but if they bring an attitude of mind that is positive and engaging they will learn quickly, with their energy flowing into others.

Grumpiness and complacency often go together. When you detect in a team a combination of grumpiness and resignation, you know that it will take a big push to galvanise them with new energy. Sometimes recruiting a couple of new people can help break up a malaise and stimulate a renewed commitment and positive outlook. New recruits need to know that they have your backing, as the positive attitude they bring may not be instantly welcomed.

When you recruit to a team you are likely to be looking for a particular type of expertise. It might be helpful to define what is the minimum level of expertise, meaning an individual is above the line for an appointment. Then select potential candidates on the basis of both aptitude for further learning and an attitude of mind, which means that they will bring an effective, galvanising approach to the overall team.

Alongside recruiting for attitude, keep a careful eye on people's attitude during their time in the role. It is important to have review arrangements that are as much about attitude and learning as they are about performance. If someone's motivation dips, it is important to be alert to the risks of disengagement and frustration sooner rather than later.

Helen was never short of applicants when she advertised posts, because of the team's reputation. She wanted to recruit people with some experience of change management: they needed to know enough about the IT world to be able to communicate effectively with other IT professionals. She needed people who would learn quickly and not flounder.

Helen was direct in the questions she asked applicants in identifying how they had learned in different situations, and what their attitude would be if things went wrong or they were criticised. She wanted to appoint people who were keen to learn, had a clear sense of responsibility, were calm under pressure and worked effectively in teams.

## In practice

- Be clear which attitudes are most important in your team.

- Think through how you will assess people for attitude and not just competence.

- Review people's attitude on a regular basis, encouraging them to maintain a balance between being positive and forward-looking and bringing candid realism.

# 78 SPOT AND FILL GAPS

EFFECTIVE TEAMS WILL BE adaptable, but there are times when potential gaps need to be spotted and filled.

## The idea

A team that is working well will include a mix of skills and approaches. When there is an issue to be addressed, team members will be ready with a range of different ideas and approaches. The astute team leader will have appointed people with different personalities and experience, so that they are complementary in what they bring to discussions and expand each other's knowledge and insight. The effective team will be adapting all the time, as individuals grow in understanding and the demands of the project evolve.

If there is a gap in expertise, the reaction of a team that is working well may well be to cover the gap. The risk is that they believe adaption is virtuous, when a hard-headed approach would lead them to be seeking new expertise within the team. Alongside spotting and filling a gap in expertise, there could be an acknowledgement that there is an excess of expertise in one area that needs reducing and adding capability in another. A gap that needs to be filled may be about a particular expertise, or it may be about adding someone who looks at issues differently and can bring freshness and curiosity to the team.

Helen was conscious that her team were predominantly men of a certain age. Her ideal was to create a team that was more diverse in terms of gender, age and cultural backgrounds. When posts were advertised, she stressed the opportunity for people to work flexibly and the scope for learning from team members with extensive experience. She made sure that the roles were advertised through networks that brought together people interested in job-share working. She appointed a couple of job shares to the team and recruited a few younger people from culturally different backgrounds, changing her team into something that was more representative of wider society.

Helen was relentless in looking ahead at what were the likely skills she was going to need in six months' time. She based her recruitment much more on what she would need in the future rather than what was instantly required.

## In practice

- Be objective in identifying potential, future gaps in expertise.

- Be honest if your team is one dimensional in the approach it brings and look to refresh the team as opportunity arises.

- Praise adaptability, but be wary if this means that fundamental issues are not tackled.

# KEEP BUILDING THE CAPABILITY AND RESILIENCE OF TEAMS

BUILDING THE CAPABILITY AND resilience of teams is a never-ending process that requires constant vigilance.

## The idea

In our Praesta Insight booklet, 'The Resilient Team', Hilary Douglas and I observed that the teams that stay resilient have the following characteristics:

- Know what the team is for and what can only be done by the team together.
- Balance planning for the longer term and dealing with the here and now.
- Work together to turn plans into reality.
- Are pro-active in response to a changing environment.
- Pay attention to values and behaviours.
- Engage effectively with stakeholders.
- Build capability for sustainable change within the organisation.
- Understand and apply effective governance.
- Maintain momentum as team members change.
- Look after their own well-being.

I recently asked all the members of a leadership team to identify three from the ten characteristics listed where the team needed to do further work. The resulting aggregated pattern of votes showed three areas where thinking and action was needed. For this team, the main priority was further work on balancing planning in the longer term while dealing with the here and now. They also wanted to work more on understanding and applying effective governance, and maintaining momentum as team members changed.

Using the checklist above provides a good basis for teams to self-assess where they are in terms of building resilience and what their next steps might be. In another team there was a particular concern about engaging effectively with stakeholders. The ensuing conversation demonstrated the timeliness of building effective links with stakeholders. It was clear that this aspiration was not corporately owned, so they agreed which stakeholders should become their priority for forward-looking conversations.

When Helen used the 10 criteria as a self-assessment tool with her team, their areas for priority attention were about working together to turn plans into reality and building capability for sustainable change in the organisation. Helen had thought the team was working well; but the fact that there was a consistent view that the team needed to work more closely together to turn plans into reality was a wake-up call for Helen. Helen felt she had been investing in building capability for sustainable change in the organisation. The fact that the team thought this strand needed to be given higher priority gave Helen a new impetus to push this theme.

## In practice

- Keep a careful eye on what might be building up or eroding the resilience of the team.

- Be systematic in assessing what is helping the team be resilient and what might be undermining that resilience.

- Encourage open conversation among team members about the characteristics of resilient teams, using approaches such as the 10 criteria listed above.

# ENCOURAGE PEOPLE TO BE CURIOUS

CURIOSITY IS A HUGELY valuable asset in any organisation.

## The idea

Curiosity may have 'killed the cat', but curiosity is an essential attribute in anyone leading transformation. The questions 'why' and 'how' are critical tools for anyone seeking to ensure that transformation leads to positive change. Exploring why current arrangements are suboptimal gives insights about what not to replicate. Intelligence about what works well in other organisations provides data about what could be possible. Looking at the lessons learned in one type of organisation or culture can provide a new angle about what might work in a different context.

Innovative organisations often give licence to people to spend work time visiting different types of companies or organisations. A family friend has recently joined a sports marketing organisation that funds each employee to participate in a sport of their choice. Their belief is that if an employee is engaged in learning and developing a sporting expertise, then that insight will flow back into their contribution to marketing the sports organisation. Employees are expected to be curious about why teams are engaged in particular sports and what motivates them, so that this understanding can be built into the way they contribute to the organisation's future thinking about marketing.

Encouraging curiosity is about understanding what makes people tick as well as how processes or technology are working. The more interested or curious someone is about how different clients or stakeholders are going to react, the more effort they are likely to put into building their engagement with these individuals. This changes the relationship from being purely transactional into something more creative and transformational.

Helen kept encouraging her people to be curious about why certain approaches worked or did not work. Curiosity involves seeing possibilities from different perspectives. It involves being forensic in understanding why some ways of working are so embedded, with the resulting difficult in changing deeply held assumptions. Helen encouraged her team leaders to reward curiosity and share examples of insights from other organisations.

## In practice

- Legitimise your own sense of curiosity. Never see it as an indulgence or a diversion.

- Enter situations where you can be deliberately curious about why and how processes work effectively.

- Be explicit in encouraging and rewarding curiosity.

- Legitimise time spent by team members exploring what they feel curious about.

# SECTION P
# KEEP THE ENERGY HIGH

# RECOGNISE SIGNS OF FATIGUE AND STALENESS

Be alert to the effects of fatigue and staleness and how different people handle continuous pressure.

## The idea

A repeated refrain from some people is that they are always tired. You become immune to their comments and find it difficult to distinguish when their tiredness is becoming acute. For others it is a matter of pride that they never describe themselves as tired, however they might be feeling. When you have worked with someone for a while you recognise the signs of fatigue, such as when certain things get forgotten or the quality of the product is not at its normal level. Many people are good at hiding their fatigue until it becomes acute and they become sick.

It can be helpful to observe people's level of energy or fatigue over the cycle of a week or in different sorts of settings. This helps build up a picture of when someone is more at risk of becoming fatigued. It can also be helpful to ask members of a team what gives them energy, and how they ensure that these activities are spread throughout a week or month in order to counter periods of tiredness.

It can be a helpful starter for discussion to invite people to say where they are on a scale of 1–10 between staleness and freshness. This can lead into a conversation about what would need to happen for the score to shift toward freshness rather than staleness.

There are times when you are going to require your team members to work especially hard because of deadlines and external expectations.

You will want to recognise the potential effect on their energy levels and well-being and make sure there is some counterbalance to ensure there are no detrimental effects from long-term pressures.

Bob was the leader for a major regeneration programme in an industrial city. There were large sections of industrial wasteland that were ripe for new usage as they were close to excellent transport links. Bob built a team of people with excellent programme management and technical skills. They 'caught the vision' and were committed to the success of the programme.

Bob was conscious that this would be a long haul spead over a number of years. He expected a lot from his team leaders, but knew that he would have to ensure that they looked after themselves and kept themselves fresh. He insisted that staff took their holidays. He encouraged them to do physically healthy activities outside work. He ensured that they had the time available to visit similar programmes elsewhere in the country, in order to pick up ideas and stave off the risk of staleness.

## In practice

- Recognise that people will either describe or hide fatigue in different ways.

- Be deliberate in opening up conversations about levels of staleness or freshness.

- When you notice someone becoming fatigued, talk to them about what might be the cause and what could help them move forward.

# UNDERSTAND THE STIMULUS NEEDED TO KEEP ENGAGEMENT HIGH

WHAT MATTERS MOST IS the quality and not just the quantity of engagement.

## The idea

Teams that spend a lot of time together can reach a point at which they become bored and frustrated. The backlash can be that so much time is spent in team meetings that the necessary work never happens, or is done poorly. Perhaps a more frequent complaint is that the team never meets together in order to have conversations: it is always rushed, transactional and uncreative.

Good quality engagement requires a level of mutual understanding and respect that comes from meeting colleagues and partners regularly without being forced to be in each other's space for excessive periods of time.

If team events are to become the highlight rather than the low point of the month there needs to be a strong underlying belief in the value of them working together and evidence of where constructive dialogue has led to better outcomes. Strong engagement flows from common purpose, a sense of shared endeavour and a belief in joint collaboration being more effective than independent action.

It is easy to let engagement slip with different stakeholders. You might assume they are aligned, when actually priorities might be moving in a different direction. Continually 'checking in' with those who have a shared interest about the success of different initiatives helps you keep tabs on whether the level of alignment is as you had hoped. Checking the levels of engagement might mean occasional phone calls or a meeting for a quick cup of coffee. A risk is that you set the expectation high in terms of how much time needs to be set aside for this, when periodic, short interchanges are what is needed.

Bob recognised that his team members were focused on their individual projects. It was important that each of them recognised that they were part of an overall programme. He insisted on regular meetings of the programme board, which he kept relatively brief. What mattered was identifying cross-cutting issues and opportunities that affected all the projects. He wanted each team member to feel they were contributing to the success of the overall venture, without feeling overburdened by central bureaucracy.

Bob was conscious that local politicians had their own agendas and could unexpectedly make unhelpful utterances. He knew he had to keep close to influential politicians and have the type of relationship where he could have private conversations with them to help forestall unhelpful public reactions from them. He had to tread a fine line between openness with politicians and ensuring that he and the team made announcements when they were ready, while minimising the risk of politicians hijacking announcements.

## In practice

- Be deliberate in ensuring good quality engagement within your team in terms of selecting topics for shared conversation.

- Be deliberate in setting expectations about how much time team members spend together, so it is productive and not excessive.

- Allocate time in a focused way to ensure effective engagement with all relevant partners and stakeholders.

# BE MINDFUL OF THE HYGIENE FACTORS

No one notices the hygiene factors until they go wrong.

## The idea

We do not realise how dependent we are on the availability of a good cup of coffee until it is very difficult to get one. We take a good Wi-Fi connection for granted and are put out if we can't get good internet reception. We have got used to being able to send and receive messages quickly: there is nothing more frustrating than mislaying our smartphone or tablet: you feel bereft and out of contact with the world.

On the other hand, we might have become entirely used to not having our own room in an office or dedicated desk space. We have become much more flexible in our use of space and time. Former essentials—such as your own desk, chair, mug, fixed telephone and the passing tea trolley—have become requirements belonging to a different age.

It is worth being clear what are the hygiene factors that are most important for a team or wider enterprise: effective, reliable communication; the availability of data; the minimising of bureaucracy; and responsiveness when there are problems and questions. For many people, the availability of good quality coffee is high up the list.

Hygiene factors are largely about processes and physical conditions, but they also extend to the standards of interaction, with people being open in their views, listening effectively to others and not dominating conversations. There may be a hygiene factor about how communication happens—be it written or oral—in terms of clarity, brevity, honesty and evidence-based.

Bob carefully monitored the underlying hygiene factors that were most important for the different project teams. They were not expecting grand office accommodation, but they did expect high quality Wi-Fi and phone connections. They wanted a break-out space where they could meet in small groups and access good-quality coffee. Bob ensured that there were people in his organisation who understood that they needed to keep an eye on the hygiene factors that were most important and to ensure a quick response when there were problems. This was not about meeting the whims of specific individuals: it was about being alert to potential niggles at an early stage so that potential frustrations were fixed before they grew.

## In practice

- See underlying hygiene factors as key to maintaining a positive spirit in a team.

- Be relentless in ensuring problems in hygiene practice are addressed.

- Accept that today's hygiene factors may be very different to those of a few years ago.

# 84 · DELEGATE RESPONSIBILITY WHENEVER YOU CAN

WELCOME THE WILLINGNESS OF people to take responsibility and allow them the scope to embrace that responsibility.

## The idea

We have reached the level we are at in an organisation because we have been prepared to take responsibility and have delivered outcomes that have been recognised by others. But success in leading teams comes through enabling others to take up the responsibility that we previously would have held. It is when we move from rowing to steering that we move into a different leadership space. The cox has a responsibility to steer the boat, but it is the rowers who have accepted the responsibility to propel the boat as fast as they possibly can. There is a shared accountability for the success of the boat, with fully delegated responsibility to the team members.

Delegation of responsibility is dereliction of duty. It involves keeping a careful watch of what is happening and providing guidance at key moments. It involves carefully preparing individuals by enabling them to learn through gradually taking on more responsibility.

It can be worth starting with a question: what is it only I can do to ensure the success of this enterprise? Answering that question will allow you to identify where you have a personal responsibility, opening up opportunities to recruit and promote particular individuals for other roles. Anything that does not fall within this limited definition of things that are your responsibility can, in principle, be delegated to others. If you do not want to delegate responsibilities to others, it is worth asking yourself what is the source of this inhibition.

Bob recognised that his key responsibility was related to ensuring clear, forward direction and adequacy of resources, the appointment of the right people and the effectiveness of key stakeholder relations. When he appointed people he had the responsibility for setting clear expectations and ensuring their effective development. He steered them at the beginning, but then was clear that the different project leaders had to take full responsibility for next steps. He involved himself for a limited length of time and then set them free. He ensured periodic reviews against expectations, but was deliberate in not usurping the responsibility he had given to the project leaders.

## In practice

- Be explicit about what are the responsibilities that only you can carry.

- Recognise your leadership journey from rowing to steering and be mindful that you do not go backwards in your approach.

- Keep pushing down responsibility, linking it with agreed sets of expectations and review points.

- Affirm those who have taken full responsibility and be specific about what you most appreciate about what they have done.

# KEEP WATCHING, OBSERVING AND RESPONDING

WE THINK THAT 'DOING' is virtuous and 'watching' is indulgent, but for a leader watching can be virtuous and doing indulgent.

## The idea

We want to keep active at making a difference. We pride ourselves on getting things done. We want to be setting a good example by rolling up our sleeves and ensuring that progress is made. We need to move on from the feeling that doing is always virtuous. If we are doing the action, we are stopping someone else from having that opportunity and experience.

Setting aside time to watch and observe allows us to view the work of the team from a different perspective. We want to observe what a team is doing from the perspective of different interests. What do clients, customers or partners think is working well—or less well— as a programme of change unfolds? What are the pressure points that are only visible if you view progress from different angles?

When I was a director general in a government department I once spent a couple of hours incognito, delivering the post to a part of the office building. I observed the range of different activities and behaviours. I was struck by the diligence of some and the lackadaisical approach of others. I was conscious that as a postman I was ignored and treated with disdain. I learned more in those two hours about what needed to happen to the culture in the organisation than I would have done through a sequence of formal meetings.

Responding to what we observe may be about asking questions or pointing out apparent contradictions. The heavy boot of authority is always available to us, but when we point out contradictions, or issues that are not being fully addressed, we can often leave the consequential review and any decisions on action to others, once they have thought through what might be an appropriate response.

Bob took time to visit the different sites where project teams were working. He deliberately talked with contractors, members of the public, community groups and politicians. He observed their behaviours and listened to their words. His use of open questions provided him with a wealth of responses. He did not promise instant action: he fed back what he saw to the relevant team leaders, asking questions and offering different possible options—but deliberately did not impose decisions on next steps. After Bob had been doing his visits and conversations the team leaders knew he would return with insights that they should not ignore.

## In practice

- Allocate time for watching and observing.

- Be as incognito as possible as you build an understanding about the workings of your organisation and its people.

- Be careful that you do not respond in a way that undermines the day-to-day responsibility of individual team leaders.

- Hold back when your initial reaction is to take control and check yourself as to whether that is the right course of action.

# SECTION Q
# EVOLVE THE NARRATIVE

# KNOW THE STORIES THAT PEOPLE ARE TELLING EACH OTHER

STORIES ARE MUCH MORE influential than bullet points.

## The idea

Families will often have a bank of stories that they share about times in the past. Teams will often share stories about events and incidents that have shaped the team. The best-remembered stories are those that were humorous or include a poignant message that team members are happy to remind themselves of.

For some, telling stories about the past is indulgent and excludes new members to a team. A team that welcomes new members explains the significance of previous stories and will be creating new stories that include the new members of the team. A team that is telling each other stories from a few years ago is in danger of looking to the past rather than the future, while a team that keeps adding new stories is demonstrating vibrancy and its sense of progress.

It is helpful to know what stories people are telling each other within an organisation. What are they describing as the high points or the low points? What stories are they are telling about your impact as a leader? When you hear the stories people are telling about you, it might provide insights about some of your foibles or approaches that people find amusing or which irritate them. These stories might also reveal in what way people are particularly engaged by your approach.

When you learn about the stories people tell about different teams, you can pick up an undercurrent about where links are warm and positive and where there might be some suspicion or unease. When there have been acts of kindness and support for people in difficulties, these often become part of the folklore about individuals. Thoughtful support during tough times is often reflected in positive stories about the way individuals have intervened in a constructive way.

Keeping an ear for the gossip will tell you a lot about what people really think; but gossip can be based on a limited viewpoint, so gossip alone rarely gives a complete picture.

Bob recognised that some individuals would share with him the gossip that was passing around the organisation. He would always listen to those stories, but would triangulate the perspectives he heard. The stories gave him insight into what was engaging and concerning people. Bob recognised the power of gossip and would sometimes deliberately feed in positive comments about people's approaches and behaviours, knowing that these comments would be disseminated through a network. He very deliberately never expressed negative comments about people to the conveyors of gossip.

## In practice

● Listen out for the stories people are telling each other.

● Encourage the telling of stories about the contribution of the team and the learning of the team.

● Prompt good gossip about people through the organisation.

● Seek to find out and learn from the stories people are telling about you.

# KEEP THE RATIONALE FOR CHANGE CLEAR, UNAMBIGUOUS AND REPEAT IT

EVEN THOUGH YOU MAY be bored with the rationale for change, keep repeating it unambiguously.

## The idea

The founder of Methodism, John Wesley, would preach the same sermon numerous times a day as he travelled through industrial England. His rationale for change was clear. People needed to be redeemed and have new hope and life, believing in Jesus Christ as Lord. This repeated message transformed lives and enabled many to escape drunkenness and squalor. John Wesley had a clear rationale about what needed to change in people's lives. He was unambiguous and repeated the same message thousands of times. What motivated him was a strong personal belief in his faith and evidence of changed lives for the better.

When you are handling rapid change, having a clear rationale brings clarity to your message and demonstrates commitment in what you are seeking to achieve. When others try to obfuscate or push you in different directions, focusing clearly on the rationale for change helps maintain momentum. Maintaining an unambiguous rationale for change does not mean being rigid about how things are done and resisting adaption. It does mean knowing why you are on a particular course of action and being able to explain this course clearly and persuasively to anybody who asks.

John Wesley never got bored with his message, because he believed he had a calling to change people's lives. When you have a leadership role in a change programme it greatly helps if you are convinced about the merits of the change, or at least can articulate the merits of the change in readily understandable ways. Repeating the same message is a necessary part of effective leadership, with your tone and your examples being moderated to fit a particular context and audience.

Bob thought it was self-evident that regeneration was important for his northern region. But there are always critics of spending money on major, capital projects. Some critics thought all investment should be in short-term, palliative measures. Bob needed to keep repeating messages about the importance of long-term investment to create sustainable jobs, so that people wanted to live and work in areas that had become industrial wastelands. His rationale was both economic and environmental, with a strong focus on the new employment opportunities that would flow. Bob was relentlessly positive about the outcomes the programme was seeking to achieve. When speaking to different groups he used illustrations and evidence relevant to that community or sector, but he never diluted the overall message.

## In practice

- Know intimately the rational for the change you are leading.

- Be unashamed in setting out that rationale, even when you have critics.

- Keep repeating the rationale, even though you are bored with it: try to make it sound fresh each time.

# ENSURE THE NARRATIVE IS UP-TO-DATE AND RELEVANT

THE RATIONALE FOR CHANGE may be unaltered, but the narrative about progress and opportunity needs to be continually updated.

## The idea

There is a distinction between the underlying rationale for change and the ongoing narrative about progress and opportunities. It is helpful to keep these two elements separate in your mind. The rationale needs to be memorable, clear, persuasive and brief. The forward narrative is a dynamic account of what is happening and how progress is being made. The narrative needs to demonstrate that listening is a continuous process, with adaptions being built in and concerns responded to.

A good narrative will include hard evidence of facts and perspectives of those influenced by the changes. A good narrative is adapted to take account of the audience. Specialists might need hard evidence of technical progress. Politicians or community leaders will need to be reassured that different perspectives are being taken into account.

New interest groups might have been formed or a new company might be thinking of providing competition. The narrative needs to be dynamic and take account of appeals being disseminated through social media or views being expressed by different community and political leaders. Sometimes it might mean taking the initiative and surveying different groups to see how expectations and attitudes are changing. You want to find out what is bubbling below the surface so you can address an issue before it turns into an emotive problem.

Bob was aware that local elections were due to take place and he was conscious of the issues that would be at the centre of the election campaign. Bob was deliberate in not taking sides, but he ensured that the narrative espoused by his organisation addressed the type of issues that the different political parties were raising. He wanted to ensure that no local party could say that he and his organisation were not listening. Bob was also conscious that a couple of Japanese companies were thinking of investing in the region. He ensured that his narrative demonstrated that they would be welcome investors who would receive practical support if they chose to invest in areas that were being regenerated. Bob sought to understand what would be most important to these Japanese investors and adapted his narrative to respond to their cultural preferences.

## In practice

- Keep your narrative updated with recent examples and stories.

- Ensure your narrative focuses on the future and not on the past.

- Understand how your narrative will be perceived by different groups.

- Provide data and stories that can be deployed by a range of people who have an interest in the outcomes of the transformation you are seeking to deliver.

# AVOID NARRATIVE CHURN

---

NEVER CHANGE A NARRATIVE just because you are bored with it.

---

## The idea

Leaders who build followers keep their rationale for change clear, ensure the narrative is up-to-date and relevant and avoid churning a narrative over and over. We may enjoy playing with words and describing approaches and next steps in a variety of different ways. For some, this sense of variety is stimulating and engaging. For others it is confusing and dispiriting.

One person I worked with was so intellectually curious and so eloquent with words that the narrative about the change he was leading was expressed differently each week. This individual was entertaining to be with, but we were wary of where he was about to take us and whether his narrative would change radically again in two weeks.

If a leader describes a possibility as good one week and then weak the next week, we may be amused but are unlikely to be inspired. If different approaches are churning around in our head we will want to talk them through with trusted others, having carefully set a broad context for these discussions. When ideas are churning we need to engage with those ideas in ourselves and other people, but need to be wary of signals we give to colleagues, who may interpret everything we say as an instruction.

When some are sceptical about the changes, it is right to think through a range of different approaches to address those concerns. We may explore alternative approaches, but this is best done deliberately and not in a way that implies that chaos and uncertainty are dominating our thinking.

Bob recognised that in order to build support and goodwill across business, politics and local communities, he needed to be clear and adaptable. He needed to give consistent messages adapted to particular groups. He also knew that it was important that he was not pushed around by strong voices. He was not going to be bullied into redefining his narrative every week to meet the needs of particular vociferous interest groups.

Bob was conscious that all the leaders in the organisation needed to be consistent in their messaging. Therefore, if he kept churning the narrative his colleagues would not know where they stood. Any unilateral messaging from him would risk the danger of others thinking that they could express their own idiosyncratic narrative. Bob knew that if he was to keep the team together the evolving narrative needed to be agreed and owned by the wider leadership group.

## In practice

- Recognise when you are in danger of adapting the narrative because you have been pressurised or even bullied by different groups.

- Be aware of when constructive development of the narrative turns into unnecessary narrative churn.

- Recognise that consistency and adaptability can go together, but requires careful explanation.

# EXPLAIN CAREFULLY WHEN AND WHY THE NARRATIVE HAS CHANGED

BE DELIBERATE IN MAKING changes to the narrative. Explain the reasons for these changes.

## The idea

When you are part of leading rapid change, inevitably the narrative will evolve in the light of new information. Some of the initial plans might have moved forward more quickly than others. Blockages might have become more acute than originally anticipated. There might be technical problems that have become bigger than originally expected. It might be that a group of people have welcomed the intended changes and want them to happen more quickly than originally envisaged.

Necessary adaptions to a narrative might result as much from positive developments as from problems that are more difficult to resolve. It can be helpful to describe a set of changes to a narrative in a holistic way and not to deal with each separately. Letting people know that a range of comments and new data are being considered and that adaptions to the narrative will be announced on a defined date can provide reassurance that issues are not being dealt with on a piecemeal basis.

When change to the narrative is announced, key to keeping good, forward momentum is clarity about the rationale. But where there are issues that are causing problems and delay, an updated narrative needs to address those issues and not obscure them. Where individuals or teams have made useful interventions that have helped the narrative develop, it is constructive to give credit to those people. This reinforces that the leadership is listening to views heard from a range of different quarters.

Bob was conscious that he had team leaders and teams in different locations working on different timescales. He developed a pattern of monthly communications, where he was deliberate in updating the narrative about progress and priorities. The written narrative followed a meeting with the team leaders. There were periodic meetings with all staff at different sites. Bob was deliberate in managing the process of decision-making on matters affecting the narrative, so that there was proper consultation and then effective articulation about reasons for the changes and next steps.

When he was about to change the narrative he would talk it through with a small consultative group, which included people from different parts of the organisation and from different grades. He sought the perspective of both his management team and this cross-section of people in order to ensure that changes in the narrative would be understood in the way he wanted.

## In practice

- Plan your forward timetable as far as possible and know when you are likely to update the narrative.

- Be careful that you do not keep adding changes to the narrative in an unplanned way with particular interest groups.

- Check out how changes to the narrative are likely to be received by different groups.

- Be deliberate in explaining why narrative change is taking place.

# SECTION R
# THRIVE WITH CHANGE

# 91 LOG THE PROGRESS MADE

CONTINUALLY LOGGING THE PROGRESS made gives you a new foundation on which to build.

## The idea

When you walk up a mountain slope you may think you are making little progress, but when you look back you see how far you have come. As you walk up the mountain you may be aiming for a particular viewpoint. It is then worth looking back and soaking up the view, allowing that experience to galvanise you for the next phase of the climb. As an example, when I write a book I divide up the task into sections, giving myself a series of attainable milestones. At each milestone I review the progress made and consider whether there are adjustments I need to make to the forward plan.

You and your immediate team may be conscious of the progress but senior people in the organisation, or those with an interest outside the organisation, may think little has happened. For the sake of your own reputation you want to demonstrate that you and your team have delivered. You want people to recognise the momentum that has been achieved so that they realise that it is too late to fundamentally change direction. If in due course you seek support from colleagues, you want to be able to demonstrate to them that their investment in this endeavour has been worthwhile, with significant progress achieved.

Part of logging progress involves forewarning people when it will be time for them to play their part. If the changes you are introducing mean some adjustments as a consequence, you want them to be aware of the forthcoming timetable so they are not taken by surprise. Part of logging progress involves demonstrating plenty of appreciation for those who have contributed to that progress. It is a key part of building up a bank of goodwill.

Bob was conscious that a couple of local authorities had said they would invest resources when the regeneration had reached a certain point. Bob was continually logging the progress with the local authorities so that these bodies could plan the timing of their investment. Bob was strongly focused on building effective partnerships with the local authorities, and did not want them to be taken by surprise. Part of his approach was to ensure that these local authorities felt obliged to fulfil the promises they had made earlier about matching the investment when a key milestone had been reached.

## In practice

- Be explicit about intermediate milestones and be deliberate in publicising when these milestones have been reached.

- Recognise that your reputation depends on clear evidence of good progress.

- Use statements about progress made to put pressure on other organisations to fully play their part in delivering the overall impact.

# CELEBRATE AND HAVE FUN TOGETHER

Marking key points and celebrating progress recharges energy and builds commitment.

## The idea

It is right to take work seriously. We have responsibilities. There are expectations upon us. We are paid to do a job well, or if we are volunteers, we carry the expectations of those who are funding the charity. Responsibility is a serious business.

There is no law against enjoying each other's company and having fun together. Joy should be part of work and shared endeavour. Work should not be drudgery: it should be fulfilling and joyful as far as possible. Inevitably there are aspects of work that are not joyful. At the moment when the prison officer locks up the prisoner, or the policeman puts handcuffs on a criminal or a doctor's patient dies, there is no joy. But for the prison warder, the policeman and the doctor there can be a long-term satisfaction in their work that provides fulfilment and a degree of joy.

Encouraging people to be joyful in their work is not straightforward, especially if a change programme is leading to job losses and a limitation of people's opportunities. You do not want to be having fun when redundancy notices have been served on employees. But there can still be satisfaction in the work you have been doing where, for example, it means rationalising the structure of an organisation so the chances of its survival and a potential regrowth are much increased. Engaging sceptics and critics in celebrating progress can help win them over, so they see the energy in the team and hear evidence of good progress being made.

Bob would take any opportunity to mark progress. If a contract was being signed this would be turned into a small ceremony, with the signing of the document in full view of cameras. When physical work began on a site there would be a 'sod turning' ceremony, where a dignitary would be asked to mark the occasion with a short speech. Bob would deliberately involve politicians in giving speeches so they became committed to the programme and its success.

Celebrations were always modest occasions so there could be no criticism about resources being wasted. A brief lunchtime or open-air event ensured people did not stay too long and eat and drink too much.

## In practice

- Mark milestones with a timely, non-indulgent celebration.

- Involve those on the fringe so they feel committed to the endeavour.

- Invite public or senior figures to give short speeches that will help tie them in to the success of the endeavour.

- Transmit joy rather than anxiety in your interactions with others who are part of the overall endeavour.

# 93 ARTICULATE THE BENEFITS FLOWING FROM CHANGE

CONTINUALLY EMPHASISING THE BENEFITS arising from change helps maintain momentum when the going is tough.

## The idea

In the midst of day-to-day concerns it is easy to lose sight of the benefits that will flow from change. It can be very helpful to draw attention to the benefits that similar changes have led to in different organisations. If different parts of the organisation are introducing changes at different speeds, it is worth highlighting the benefits that have flowed where the changes have already occurred.

The benefits that matter most will vary for different people. In the Finance Department it is the financial benefits that will matter most. What will matter particular to the Operations Department is whether processes can happen more efficiently and with less disruption. The HR Department might be looking at absence rates or recognition rates. Clearly visualising which benefits are going to matter most to which groups will allow you to focus on how those benefits can materialise and what is the best way of assessing those benefits.

The most powerful advocates of the benefits are those who are directly affected by the change. It is much more convincing if the customer recognises the benefits they are beginning to experience rather than being persuaded by you.

Bob was convinced that the regeneration work would be a catalyst for renewed economic activity and a reduction in the unemployment rates in the area. The initial ground-clearing work led to a first phase of jobs. Part of the contract was that the employers needed to provide training for the workforce. This improvement in the employability of people who had been long-term unemployed increased the reputation of the regeneration work. The construction work meant further jobs and development opportunities.

There was a knock-on effect in terms of local businesses providing services, such as a mobile café. Signs of economic activity increased the likelihood of further jobs being created. When a major firm decided it was going to relocate to that region because of the investment that was happening, this provided further evidence of potential, long-term benefits. Bob encouraged local employers to share platforms with him where they talked about the benefits of the regeneration work for them and their employees.

## In practice

- Be specific about the benefits that will flow from the changes.

- As soon as there are benefits, seek to identify them and broadcast them.

- Draw in partners who are directly affected by the change to talk openly about the benefits from their perspective.

- Seek to ensure that those who have grasped the opportunity that the changes provide are recognised and rewarded.

# BE EXCITED ABOUT WHAT IS GOING TO HAPPEN NEXT

THE LEADER WHO CAN always see hope and opportunity is more likely to have followers than the leader for whom the future is all gloom.

## The idea

The leader who can talk effectively about the future and be convincing in describing what is going to happen next can generate momentum among their followers, which means they will be looking for opportunities rather than being dominated by frustrations. An optimistic view of the future has to be grounded in realism. The leader who gets over-excited about future possibilities, with little supporting evidence, is unlikely to be convincing in the longer term.

If the leader of a walking group talks both about the ultimate objective and about the delights of a view up ahead, the walk leader is combining a sense of aspiration for the eventual outcome with opportunities for progress over the shorter term. The motivating leader is always lifting the veil on what might be possible in the foreseeable future. They are building a sense of excitement about what is attainable rather than focusing only on the ultimate perfect outcome.

For some people, describing a problem that needs to be cracked gives a sense of excitement about what they need to do. For others the sense of excitement flows from the team they will be working with rather than the intellectual challenge. For others there will be a quiet excitement about the small steps of progress that are possible in enabling financial and human resources to be applied more effectively.

Bob recognised that he could get over-excited about what was going to happen next and talk too much about some of the detail. Bob acknowledged that when he was in full flow he could be overpowering. On the other hand, there were people who needed the tonic of Bob in full flow in order to become fully committed to next steps.

As the overall programme grew in size Bob recognised that he could become a liability if everyone needed the tonic of his positive approach for them to move forward. He needed to recalibrate how he communicated what was going to happen next. He sought to develop his team leaders to help them communicate the sense of purposefulness and excitement that would generate commitment amongst all involved in delivering the programme.

## In practice

- When you feel excited about next steps, channel that excitement and do not squash it.

- Be willing to describe next steps and their potential impact in visual, persuasive terms.

- Build in a sense of anticipation in the way you describe next steps and draw out the implications for the whole organisation of those next steps.

- Recognise that your tone and approach will be contagious.

# 95 ENSURE THE CASUALTIES ARE LOOKED AFTER

THE GREAT MAJORITY OF change programmes create casualties. There is a duty of care to help those adversely affected by change to find a way forward.

## The idea

Effective change programmes lead to radical change. For some this will mean new opportunities to be grasped. For others it can mean disappointment and a sense of rejection and failure. Those adversely affected will go through a cycle of anger, annoyance, grief, frustration and disappointment. Their energy levels and self-esteem may dip dramatically.

For some being jolted into new ways of thinking is exactly the shock they needed. Many people will talk of the beneficial effects of change programmes that force them to reevaluate their futures. For some, a change programme will mean the end of the road in terms of promotion and sometimes employment.

What is vital in any change programme is that individuals are treated with respect. This means adequate information and a thoughtful exposition about why changes are needed and what is going to happen now. Effective, open communication done in a timely and sympathetic way can help individuals accept the inevitable.

Enabling people to keep their self-respect through proper acknowledgement of their contribution is right for both them and the organisation. Others will be watching how casualties are looked after, recognising that they could be a casualties in the future. The allocation of time and resources for retraining and the opening up of new opportunities is part of respecting the dignity of staff and acknowledging the contribution that people have made to the endeavour over previous years.

Bob recognised that he would need different skills for different phases in the work of his team. During the initial phase of clearing sites the programme needed people with skills in decontamination, but this would be for a limited period. Bob was always clear that some roles would be temporary. When a company bought a big site they decided to go straight to using their own workforce rather than the contractors that the regeneration organisation were using. This meant that some groups of workers were made redundant sooner than expected. Bob handled this situation with care, explaining to the staff what had happened and why. Ultimately, many of them were offered jobs by the employer buying the site because of the quality of expertise they were able to bring.

## In practice

- Be clear who might be the casualties of the changes you are introducing.

- Ensure that potential casualties are not ignored or forgotten in the desire to complete the programme quickly.

- Be deliberate in ensuring appropriate development, training and resettlement provision for those who are detrimentally affected.

# MOVE TO THE NEXT MOUNTAIN

# RECHARGE YOUR BATTERIES

There are moments when it is imperative to renew your energy and rest a while.

## The idea

When you are in the midst of a transformation programme you are living on adrenalin. Pace is fast-moving, with a myriad of issues to be addressed. You have learnt how to cope with tiredness and keep going because of the relentless nature of the programme you are involved in.

When a project finishes there can be a mixture of emotions, including exhilaration and exhaustion. There can be an element of grief if members of the team are moving in different directions. Often there is a sense of anti-climax. Your brain slows down and your energy dissipates. Your batteries need recharging.

This process is a normal response at the end of a demanding period. Your body and brain need a break. It is important to go with the flow and not expect to be operating at the same level of intensity. Allowing yourself to go slow for a period is in an essential part of the recovery. Fighting the slowing down can be dangerous and can lead to a period of chronic fatigue.

Recharging your batteries can be done in a number of ways. It might involve sleeping a lot, or going for long walks or cycle rides. It might mean reading some novels that you have meant to read for quite a long time. You might decide that now is the moment for a sabbatical, with the opportunity to visit and explore areas that have been on your wish list for a while. It might mean renewing friendships.

Recharging your batteries might include a number of different phases starting with rest and ending with some intense, physical activity. Sometimes you might need to go through the cycle quite quickly as you move from one role to another.

When Alex had completed the merger of the two departments at the hospital she was able to take a two-week break. She deliberately spent the first weekend with friends, catching up with them. These conversations refreshed her. She spent some time with her parents, which always gave her a warm glow as they loved her and looked after her well. She read a couple of books that had been by her bedside for a few months. There were low points when she felt exhausted, but she took huge satisfaction in the completion of the merger and began to look forward to tackling some of the issues that had been put to one side while she was leading the project.

## In practice

- Recognise the type of emotions you are likely to experience at the end of a project: enjoy the exhilaration and allow yourself to be exhausted.

- Spend time with people you value and allow their company to cheer you up.

- Be deliberate in how you spend recuperation time, balancing rest and activity.

# 97 UPDATE YOUR NARRATIVE

UPDATING YOUR CURRICULUM VITAE (CV) can feel like a chore, but it is essential for your next steps.

## The idea

We hurriedly make a few amendments to an existing text and regard it as an up-to-date CV. We might have developed a narrative describing the contribution we brought when we last went for an interview. We rehearsed the narrative so well that it is stuck in our memory. We were comfortable with that narrative when we went for a previous interview, which may now be a few years ago.

There is a risk that we stick with the narrative we are comfortable with, but which is now out of date. We need to update our narrative so it is timely, fresh and persuasive. Our narrative might say that we are good at leading project teams, with lots of examples to support this assertion, but we might have moved on with our current skills being more focused on enabling others to lead teams well. Our greatest contribution now might be enabling and steering rather than doing, but our narrative might be stuck in a time warp and not reflect our evolving contribution.

When you have completed a programme it is well worth taking stock about what was distinctive about your contribution. It is worth asking others what they observed about your impact. It can be useful to seek the perspective of people who have only known you over the last six months as their viewpoint is determined by what they have observed in you recently. Refreshing your CV and your oral narrative as you move from programme to programme keeps it up-to-date and means it is more likely to be relevant to current activities and emerging pressures.

The work Kim had done leading a programme transferring responsibility from Europe to India had helped him develop an acute understanding of different cultural perspectives. It had widened his range of influencing approaches. He was now much more confident in a wider range of different settings. He asked some of his Indian colleagues for their perspective on the contribution he had made. He was pleasantly surprised by some of their comments about his quick grasp of difficult issues. Some of his European colleagues described his approach as both direct and persuasive. Kim recognised that he had come through a confidence barrier and knew that he could now be much more challenging and direct than previously.

## In practice

- Commit time to reshaping your CV and personal narrative.

- Seek the views of people who have only known you recently about what they most appreciate in your contribution.

- Recognise how your leadership contribution has evolved; be deliberate in describing the latest version rather than an historic version.

- Beware lest you retain too much attachment to an outdated professional narrative.

# 98 | DITCH OUTDATED PERCEPTIONS

It is time to move on from perceptions about people and situations that are outdated.

## The idea

There are moments when we need to grow up and leave outdated perceptions behind. During my first 10 years working as a civil servant in the UK Government I saw myself as a Yorkshire lad having to keep up with people who were better educated and better off than me. When I worked as Principal Private Secretary to Mark Carlisle, a UK Cabinet Minister, in one frank conversation he told me firmly that I was now a member of a senior cadre and should ditch outdated perceptions about myself and others. He told me it was time to grow fully into the leadership opportunities I now had. This was a cathartic moment. I still cherish my Yorkshire roots and see them as a strength and not something to apologise for.

We can carry with us perceptions that we are not good at certain things. We may believe that we are not good at presentations. We may think that we cannot communicate effectively with certain types of people. It is worth asking whether these perceptions are out of date. What is the most recent evidence from presentations we have given, or about meetings we have had with difficult people? The recent evidence might well be much more positive than we give ourselves credit for.

If we have a perception that we are not good at chairing meetings, it is worth taking the opportunity to chair small meetings and then gradually move into chairing bigger meetings. We then build evidence that our original perception is out of date.

When Kathy reflected on how she had developed when leading the change programme in an insurance company she recognised how much her confidence had grown hugely in dealing with senior figures. Her previous perception was that senior managers were distant, analytic and cold-hearted. Her new experience of the senior managers was that they were analytic, but could also see the human as well as the financial dimensions. Once it was clear they shared the same agenda, Kathy found the leadership to be much more engaging than she had expected. Kathy needed to ditch an outdated perception that senior managers were unapproachable and cold-hearted. She had to ditch her perception of herself that she was not able to communicate effectively with senior managers at a personal level.

## In practice

- Review how your perceptions of individuals and situations have evolved.

- Be explicit in redefining how you view those in leadership positions.

- Recognise that you will be continually updating your perception of yourself and leaving behind outdated perceptions.

# KEEP AN OPEN MIND

DO NOT LET YOURSELF to be defined by the expectations of others. Keep an open mind about future possibilities.

## The idea

When you complete a project or programme you might be exhilarated and feel that you want to continue to do exactly the same sort of work going forward. On the other hand, you might conclude that you have had as much experience and exposure in a particular area as you need: you now want to take forward some very different activities. It may be that your boss or others in the organisation have seen the skills you bring and might be seeking to steer you in a particular direction. They might be identifying potential in you for particular future roles.

It is helpful to develop your own perspectives about what you might do next, taking account of the views of others. What matters is that you own the decisions about what happens next. Do not feel over-influenced about going in one particular direction or another. When you feel a weight of expectation about next steps it is important to stand back, take stock and talk to people who know you well before you make a firm decision.

Updating your narrative and ditching out-of-date perceptions can lead to new possibilities going forward. It is right to keep an open mind and explore a number of different possibilities. Even though your boss might have particular expectations, a good boss will want you to reach your own conclusions in the light of work, professional and personal considerations.

It can be helpful to think of your skills and interests in a generic way rather than linked to a specific type of job. For example, the work you have been involved in will have developed your influencing skills, hence the question becomes: how can I deploy those influencing skills in a range of different contexts effectively?

Helen took quiet satisfaction in the outcomes of the IT transformation project as individuals saw the benefits of the changes. They were very appreciative to Helen about her resolve and her willingness to push them to accept new ways of working. The day after the successful completion of the IT transformation project, Helen's boss began talking about her leading a similar project in an adjacent part of the organisation. Helen wanted to reflect on how her transformation skills could be used on a wider platform. After completing this successful project, she could seek a job in head office or lead a transformation project in an area other than IT. Perhaps the time was right to think of moving to a completely different organisation.

Helen was determined to keep an open mind and reflected on different possibilities with a couple of trusted friends, setting out clearly the pros and cons of different options. She was not going to be rushed into making a decision, as her marketability was high after this successful project.

## In practice

- Beware if the expectations of others push you in directions you do not want to go.

- Give yourself time before you make irreversible decisions about next steps.

- See your skills as generic and not limited to one type of activity or sector.

- Think into very different possibilities going forward before you narrow down the options.

# REMEMBER WHY YOU ARE THERE

ALWAYS BE CLEAR ABOUT your reasons for being where you are.

## The idea

Before you move to the next mountain it is worth reflecting on why you are where you are. Your answer will be a mixture of happenstance, choices by you and decisions by others. You may feel a victim of circumstance, or you might feel a sense of calling or vocation. Your response to why you are there might be in order to earn enough money to look after your family and pay the bills.

It can be helpful to think about why you are in a particular place in terms of the opportunity to influence people and situations constructively. You might have an inner sense of wanting to bring hope and new life into difficult situations.

Why you are in a particular situation might be to do with the shaping of your character and resolve. You might be learning a lot about your own humanity and how you are able to create communities where people are effective, fulfilled and able to develop outcomes that are for the greater good.

It may be time to move on, where the reasons for your presence may be different. There are choices to be made by you in terms of your approach and attitude. The particular task or role you do next may flow from the decisions of others, which you may have some opportunity to influence. Whatever your next role, you can choose how to draw on your previous experience, how to deploy your recent learning, and how to apply the values that are most important to you going forward.

Bob kept reminding himself that the regeneration work he was leading would result in more jobs and a better environment. He was able to see the results of his contribution in a very direct way. This gave Bob an enormous sense of personal satisfaction. When the phases of regeneration work came to an end, Bob needed to take stock about what to do next. If he led another phase of regeneration there would be the opportunity to build on what he had learnt. This would give him huge satisfaction, but for now maybe the time was right to lead a regeneration project in another part of the country.

There was a strong sense of vocation about leading regeneration, which had been strengthened by the experience of the recent programme. Bob was open to different ways of building on that sense of vocation as he looked at job possibilities and talked to a range of people he trusted.

## In practice

- Be objective in recognising that you are in a particular place because of a combination of your choices, decisions by others and happenstance.

- Reflect on any sense of vocation and how your recent experience is reinforcing that sense of calling.

- Be clear to yourself in identifying the hope and new life you can help bring to new situations.

## BOOKS BY PETER SHAW

*Mirroring Jesus as Leader.* Cambridge: Grove, 2004

*Conversation Matters: how to engage effectively with one another.* London: Continuum, 2005

*The Four Vs of Leadership: vision, values, value-added, and vitality.* Chichester: Capstone, 2006

*Finding Your Future: the second time around.* London: Darton, Longman and Todd, 2006

*Business Coaching: achieving practical results through effective engagement.* Chichester: Capstone, 2007 (co-authored with Robin Linnecar)

*Making Difficult Decisions: how to be decisive and get the business done.* Chichester: Capstone, 2008

*Deciding Well: a Christian perspective on making decisions as a leader.* Vancouver: Regent College Publishing, 2009

*Raise Your Game: how to succeed at work.* Chichester: Capstone, 2009

*Effective Christian Leaders in the Global Workplace.* Colorado Springs: Authentic/Paternoster, 2010

*Defining Moments: navigating through business and organisational life.* Basingstoke: Palgrave/Macmillan, 2010

*The Reflective Leader: standing still to move forward.* Norwich: Canterbury Press, 2011 (coauthored with Alan Smith)

*Thriving in Your Work: how to be motivated and do well in challenging times.* Singapore: Marshall Cavendish, 2011

*Getting the Balance Right: leading and managing well.* Singapore: Marshall Cavendish, 2013

*Leading in Demanding Times.* Cambridge: Grove, 2013 (co-authored with Graham Shaw)

*The Emerging Leader: stepping up in leadership.* Norwich: Canterbury Press, 2013, (coauthored with Colin Shaw)

*100 Great Personal Impact Ideas.* Singapore: Marshall Cavendish, 2013

*100 Great Coaching Ideas.* Singapore: Marshall Cavendish, 2014

*Celebrating Your Senses.* Delhi: ISPCK, 2014

*Sustaining Leadership: renewing your strength and sparkle.* Norwich: Canterbury Press, 2014

*100 Great Team Effectiveness Ideas.* Singapore: Marshall Cavendish, 2015

*Wake Up and Dream.* Norwich: Canterbury Press, 2015

*100 Great Building Success Ideas.* Singapore: Marshall Cavendish, 2016

*The Reluctant Leader: coming out of the shadows.* Norwich: Canterbury Press, 2016 (coauthored with Hilary Douglas)

*100 Great Leading Well Ideas.* Singapore: Marshall Cavendish, 2016

*Living with never-ending expectations.* Vancouver: Regent College Publishing, 2017 (coauthored with Graham Shaw)

## Forthcoming books

*The Mindful Leader: applying Christian principles.* Norwich: Canterbury Press, 2018

*Leadership to the Limits: freedom and responsibility.* Norwich: Canterbury Press, 2019

*100 Great Leading through Frustration Ideas.* Singapore: Marshall Cavendish, 2019

## Booklets

*Riding the Rapids.* London: Praesta, 2008 (coauthored with Jane Stephens)

*Seizing the Future.* London: Praesta, 2010 (coauthored with Robin Hindle-Fisher)

*Living Leadership: finding equilibrium.* London: Praesta, 2011

*The Age of Agility.* London: Praesta, 2012 (coauthored with Steve Wigzell)

*Knowing the Score: what we can learn from music and musicians.* London: Praesta, 2016 (co-authored with Ken Thompson)

*The Resilient Team.* London: Praesta, 2017 (coauthored with Hilary Douglas)

Copies of the booklets above can be downloaded from the Praesta website.

# ABOUT THE AUTHOR

Peter Shaw works with individuals, teams and groups to help them grow their strengths and tackle demanding issues confidently. His objective is to help individuals and teams to clarify their vision of what they want to be, the values that are driving them, the value-added they want to bring and their sources of vitality.

His work on how leaders step up successfully into demanding leadership roles and ustain that success was recognised with the award of a PhD by publication from the University of Chester in 2011.

Peter was a founding partner of Praesta Partners, an international specialist coaching business. His clients enjoy frank, challenging conversations, leading to fresh thinking and new insights. It is the dynamic nature of the conversations that provide a stimulus for creating reflection and new action. He often works with chief executives and board members taking on new roles and leading major organisational change. Peter has worked with a wide range of different leadership teams as they tackle new challenges.

Peter has worked with chief executives and senior teams in a range of different sectors and countries across six continents. He has led workshops on such themes as 'Riding the Rapids', 'Seizing the Future', 'Thriving in your Work', 'Being an Agile Leader' and 'Building Resilience'.

Peter has held a wide range of board posts covering finance, personnel, policy, communications and delivery. He worked in five UK government departments (Treasury, Education, Employment, Environment and Transport). He delivered major national changes, such as radically different pay arrangements for teachers, a huge expansion in nursery education and employment initiatives that helped bring UK unemployment below a million.

He led the work on the merger of the UK Government Departments of Education and Employment. As Finance Director General, he managed a £40bn budget and introduced radical changes in funding and accountability arrangements. In three Director General posts he led strategic development and implementation in major policy areas. He was awarded a CB by the Queen in 2000 for his contribution to public service.

Peter has written a sequence of 26 influential leadership books. He is a Visiting Professor of Leadership Development at Newcastle University, Chester University and De Montfort University. He has worked with senior staff at Brighton University, Edinburgh University and Herriot Watt University and postgraduate students at Warwick University Business School and Durham University. He is a member of the Visiting Professorial Faculty at Regent College in Vancouver. He is a Professorial Fellow at St John's College, Durham University. He was awarded an Honorary Doctorate (Doctor of Civil Law) by Durham University in 2015 for 'outstanding service to public life and to the Council of St. John's College'.

Peter is a Reader (licensed lay minister) in the Anglican Church and has worked with senior church leaders in the UK, North America and Asia. In December 2016 Peter was installed as a lay canon at Guildford Cathedral in recognition of his contribution to the Church of England. Peter chairs the Guildford Cathedral Council.

Peter's inspiration comes from long-distance walks, including, recently, the Machu Pichu trail in Peru. He has completed 28 long-distance walks in the UK, including the St Cuthbert's Way, the South Downs Way, the Yorkshire Wolds Way, the Yorkshire Dales Way, the Ribble Way, the Speyside Way, the St Oswald's Way, the Great Glen Way and the Westmoreland Way. Peter and his wife, Frances, have three grown up children who are all married, and a growing number of grandchildren.